Eugene Hausmann has been involved in ministry all his adult life, including more than thirty-five years as chaplain and director of pastoral care at Holy Cross Children's Services of Michigan. Much of this ministry has been ecumenical, involving diverse religious backgrounds among the clientele, the staff, and the many chaplain interns whom he trained and supervised. He was licensed to teach Science and Chemistry by the State of Michigan in 1972. Gene also served 9 years as adjunct instructor in World Religions and Social Ethics at Siena Heights University. Eugene was prepared for his ministry at Notre Dame University (where he majored in Theology and Chemistry), the Catholic Theological Union of Chicago (where he studied under the editors of *Zygon: Journal of Religion and Science*), Sacred Heart Seminary and the Ecumenical Theological Seminary of Detroit, from which he received a Doctor of Ministry degree in 2000. He was certified as chaplain in the National Association of Catholic Chaplains in 1993 and ordained deacon in the Diocese of Lansing, Michigan, in 2000. Eugene and his wife, Jean, have been married for 40 years and have three grown children and five grandchildren.

Praise for *Jobe Syndrome*...

I loved the Jobe Syndrome manuscript. I found it easy to read and the timing of the information was spot on for me. I will be faced with another treatment decision in 6 months which will be based on how accurate the doctors, MRI machines and needle biopsy are in determining if tumors are oncocytoma or carcinoma in nature...

As I face my own medical problems and not letting myself acquire Jobe Syndrome, your book has strengthened my faith. I've seen the "Jobe Syndrome" first-hand in my confirmation sponsor. I was confirmed in college in the early 1980s and my sponsor was another student earning a BSEE degree. She is a very smart person. She had recently lost her brother in the early 1980s to MS and he left behind a young widow and small children. She couldn't understand why God would let that happen. I've struggled with providing her an answer; nothing I told her provided her any comfort. I wish I could have told her that God let his son die a painful death on a cross—that Jesus cried when he was on earth—that he has sent his Holy Spirit to be with us. I think everyone has struggled with Jobe Syndrome—few provide any answers.

Your book has taken many ideas that I had over my life struggling with providing answers to friends and family on why God seems to have abandoned them? Is there a God? The concept of sincere Love for God is what he has designed the earth to produce is an idea that I had developed as an answer—your writings have reinforced my thoughts on this. They have brought together many fragmented pieces of my education, both intellectual and spiritual, in one place—almost like you wrote this book for me! You have also introduced me to additional concepts that I did not know about in the Atheist vs Theist debate… Thank you for sharing your manuscript with me. You have touched my life with it.

Robert J Cencer, Professional Engineer

Robert is a cradle to grave Catholic. He has a Bachelor of Science in Mechanical Engineering (BSME) from Michigan Technological University and a Master of Science in Administration from Central Michigan University. He is a Professional Engineer licensed in Michigan. Bob has worked in various technical fields for the past 36 years. Bob is listed on 20 US Patents. He was a Cub Master and an Assistant Scout Master and he is a member of the Knights of Columbus. He is married with four children and 2 grandchildren.

Before I actually read a book, I usually check out the back of the book. It was obvious you had done a tremendous amount of research for this book. From your Index, Appendices A & B, and Endnotes, I was impressed with the material used to write and argue your position.

I enjoyed reviewing and learning the various "fields"–gravitational, electromagnetic, strong nuclear, weak nuclear, and bio. I valued your solid analysis comparing entropy and anthropy in your argument of an Intelligent Designer, God. Your "Five

Gaps in Scientific Knowledge" analysis vs natural law was outstanding. Your chapters on Sun, Moon, Earth, Water, Wind, Air, and Fire were important in the argument for God.

Actually, each section of the entire book was noteworthy as it moves the reader through the premise for the existence of God. Your Epilogue of God speaking to Jobe was a brilliant way of summarizing your key points in the manuscript.

I do not have any constructive criticism to improve the manuscript. I truly enjoyed reading it. You're right–it's not the usual kind of spiritual reading. But, for those who question the existence of God, it is a MUST read. Actually, it's a MUST read for believers to strengthen their faith and help them argue the existence of God. The book could be considered a foundational level of Apologetics, where the existence of God is decisively defended.

Thanks for sharing your manuscript with me.

Philip Cousino

At Chrysler Corporation, Phil Cousino had lead assignments in Design/Development Engineering, Vehicle Development, and Scientific Labs/Proving Grounds. His most recent Engineering positions, prior to retirement in 2008, included Chief Engineer–2005 Jeep Grand Cherokee & Jeep Commander and Chassis Director–Jeep & Large Car Platforms.

Phil Cousino received his Engineering degree from Michigan State University with post graduate courses from the University of

Detroit-Mercy. Post retirement, Phil Cousino has been active in his Catholic Parish and School.

I've read your book and need to congratulate you on a significant theological work that is generally well-documented with impressive logical and philosophical thoughts. The chapters on scientific evidence for an Intelligent Designer were especially good.

I still struggle with your arguments for Original Sin. God created man with free will and knowing that selfishness (present in all creation) would influence free will. So there is no alternative world that could have been chosen that would not involve selfishness. There is no plausible "perfect world" where no selfish acts would occur. How could the world exist without pain and suffering? God, the intelligent designer, owns his creation, the selfish human, good and bad…

Charles T Hausmann BSE University of Detroit, MS in Agricultural Engineering (1976), Michigan State University. Founding partner of Matrix Consulting Engineers, Lansing, Michigan. Cradle Catholic, married 52 years with 3 children and 5 grandchildren.

EUGENE HAUSMANN

JOBE
SYNDROME

and Scientific Evidence for the
Existence of God and Evil

XULON PRESS

Xulon Press
2301 Lucien Way #415
Maitland, FL 32751
407.339.4217
www.xulonpress.com

Printed with Ecclesiastical Permission.
Most Reverend Earl Boyea. August 10, 2020
Lansing, Michigan

Printed in the United States of America.

Paperback ISBN-13: 978-1-6628-0039-9
eBook ISBN-13: 978-1-6628-0040-5

To my son, John,
Who has been an outstanding science teacher
And an outstanding Catholic Christian

Acknowledgements

To Deacon Engineer Carl Boehlert, the first person to review my manuscript.

To Engineers Robert Cencer, Philip Cousino, Jim Douglas and Charles Hausmann who have reviewed my manuscript with love.

To Fr. Pieter van Rooyen who assisted me with theological orthodoxy

To Aaron Mantyla, the first Millennial to read my manuscript

To Jeremy Burke, who offered his editing skills.

To Raymond Welsh, who shared his gift of scratchboard art on the front cover of this book.

To Sarie Dermanelian, Cynthia Van Pelt, Fr. Tim Nelson, who gave me valuable feedback on *Jobe Syndrome*.

To Jean and Dawn, who read my manuscript out of love

Table of Contents

Foreword

There was a time I had doubted that God was real. I had contemplated the "what if" of Him not existing. Of all of religion being made up. Of me being a sucker for continuing to go to church each week. I've contemplated people questioning my beliefs and judging me by those differences that we have.

As an adult, I consider it healthy to question things of all sorts: people, personal or political beliefs, politicians, opposing viewpoints, my kids' dietary decisions. Why not question God and His existence?

Many modern scholars have been out to disprove God's existence. They've made it their life's work to do so. Their works are filled with theories on how the world began, how women and men have evolved from apes, and how little room there is to believe that God created all of what we see and experience in life. For some of these scholars, there is such a strong conviction that God is man-made. For others, their agnostic viewpoint allows room for the possibility of God's existence.

I'm a millennial. Whether I hate it or love it, if I Google "millennial," I fall into that birth range of years. I've observed other millennials around me for quite a while now, and I'm constantly trying to make sense of the current world we live in. I can tell you from experience that there's not a lot of God-talk happening. Affirmation from others seems to be the religion of today. In today's world, how many likes (👍) we get is what matters. When someone posts a selfie on Instagram, people want their friends to reassure them that they're beautiful, that they're strong, that they're still relevant. That the depression they're feeling is normal. That it's okay to fumble our way through parenting; who doesn't? We want people to know that Black Lives Matter, that Love is Love, and that Science is Real.

Science is real. Science is real. Science is real.

Yes, science is real! But why can't Science AND God be real? Seems like it's an either/or. Science or God. Which side are you on? Are you scientific? Or are you religious? But what if science didn't actually end up disproving God? What if it supported the existence of God? I think God loves science! I think God thinks biology is cool. I think human anatomy is His favorite subject, because, as Christians believe, we were created in His "image and likeness." Science and God: like love and marriage, you can't have one without the other.

But still we choose, now more than ever, to go our own way. People today always seem to say, "You do you." I feel like I hear "you do you" a LOT. And what's good for you may not necessarily be what's good for me, and that's okay. I like things my way and you like things your way, and that's okay. We want what's easy...let's push the easy button! What's easy? Being non-judgmental. Not stepping on anyone's toes. And for some odd reason, while all this is happening, we seem to have a mental health crisis on our hands. Rates of depression continue to increase, we've found ourselves in the middle of an opioid drug epidemic in America, and antidepressant use is on the rise. Maybe it's time to give God another chance.

I was recently emailed a transcript that was written and spoken by the late great radio host, Paul Harvey, entitled, *If I were the Devil.* Mr. Harvey, depicting the devil, lays out his plans for the world. It's incredibly prophetic, being that it's written and spoken in 1965, years before many of the "actions" of the devil would actually be executed. Here are a few lines from the letter:

> *"To the young I would whisper that the Bible is a myth. I would convince them that man created God instead of the other way around. I would confide that what is bad is good, and what is good is 'square'."*[1]

The book you're about to read will offer you the strong possibility, if not the certainty, that God is real. It will highlight gaps in atheistic theories. It will show how unlikely are the probabilities that we, and the Earth we live on, "just happened." It will challenge you to consider where "Love" originated in a world where survival of the fittest is a dominant viewpoint. To the theists reading this book, allow this book to be ammunition you need in the world today to stand up and argue for the existence of a Supreme Being. If you're a non-believer, continue reading with an open mind to the possibility of there being something more. We are more than just an accident.

---

[1] https://www.youtube.com/watch?v=QGrWvrGDOXg

John Hausmann, BA in Education with Integrated Sciences Concentration

Owner of Hausmann Homes, Charlotte, NC

Introduction

On April 7, 2019, The Daily Wire[1] reported that the General Social Survey (GSS)[2] data from 2018 showed that "For the first time in history, atheists constitute the largest religious group in America... and now account for 23.1% of the population, just barely edging out Catholics and Evangelicals as the nation's dominant faith." This seems to climax a trend of the past 30 years. Ironically, this trend seems to fly in the face of science: "Science increasingly makes the case for God" is the title of the *Wall Street Journal* article by Eric Metaxas, published on Christmas day, 2014. By March 25, 2015, the Journal claimed that it was "the most popular article in *Wall Street Journal* history".[3] Why the disconnect?

I believe the confusion is caused by the universities whose world views come from 19th century and early 20th century science—and their students are learning it. The great thinkers of that period like Darwin (creation without a creator), Marx (government without religion), Freud (psychology without a soul) and Nietzsche ("God is Dead")—they have been most influential in university world views. On the other hand, the science of the late 20th century and 21st century has not been sufficiently disseminated and digested in the Millennial culture of our time. The purpose of the Metaxas article—and the purpose of this book—is to bring some of this newer science to light in a readable, non-technical format and to open the eyes of our culture to the Intelligent Design of the Universe.

Metaxas mentions the astronomer, the late Carl Sagan, who announced in 1966 that there were two criteria for a planet like earth to support life: the right star and a planet the right distance from the star. Sagan estimated that there were trillions of planets in the universe capable of (creating and) supporting life.

> As our knowledge of the universe increased, it became clear that there were far more factors necessary for life than Sagan supposed. His two parameters grew to 10 and then 20 and then 50, and so the number of potentially life-supporting planets decreased accordingly. The number dropped to a few thousand planets and kept on plummeting... As factors continued to be discovered, the number of possible planets hit zero, and kept going... Today there are more than 200 known parameters necessary for a planet to support life—every single one of which must be perfectly met, or the whole thing falls apart.[4]

Metaxas also mentions some key scientists who are more open to religious answers—Fred Hoyle, Paul Davies and John Lennox. He quotes "Oxford professor" Dr. Lennox:

> "the more we get to know about our universe, the more that the hypothesis that there is a

Creator…gains in credibility as the best explanation of why we are here."[5]

There is a growing number of scientists who are admitting that Darwinian evolution theory does not fully explain the origin of life. There are more than 500 scientists worldwide that have signed "A Scientific Dissent from Darwinism," including at least three from the University of Michigan:

> [Ronald] Larson says "that evidence for natural spontaneous formation of living cells from undirected chemical reactions is virtually non-existent."

> [Kenneth] Ludema…cites the minute mathematical probability that such elaborate structures could emerge from random processes… It begs for other explanations." [Phillip] Savage said he signed the petition because there are those who are trying to assert the origin of life has been fully established scientifically when in fact the evidence does not support that.[6]

Perhaps the most recent dissenter from Darwinism is the "renowned writer and Yale University professor" David Gelernter:

> Try to mutate your way from 150 links of gibberish to a working, useful protein and you are guaranteed to fail. Try it with ten mutations, a thousand, a million—you fail. The odds bury you. It can't be done."

Though he doesn't personally subscribe to the theory of intelligent design, Gelernter said it is an "absolutely serious argument," noting that it is the "first, and obviously most intuitive [theory] that comes to mind…" [7]

Intelligent design is the missing link in evolution theory. Without it, the odds against the random mutations and natural selection producing the complexity of a living cell are insurmountable. With intelligent design and the Designer's language embedded in the DNA of every living cell, evolution can become possible.

As a young college student at Notre Dame in the 1960's, I discovered Fr. Teilhard de Chardin,[8] a Jesuit Paleontologist who endorsed evolution theory as the method God used to create all living things and especially, human beings. His blending of modern science and theology struck me as a contemporary version of what St. Thomas Aquinas had done in the 13th century—the harmonizing of theology with science. I was fascinated and inspired. I went on to complete a double major in Theology and Chemistry and Teilhard continued to inspire my faith in the harmony of science and religion. I didn't get interested in the Biblical book of Job (pronounced "Jobe") until I became a chaplain for troubled youth in 1981. Suddenly I was inundated with kids who had been through what Jobe had been through—violent deaths, abuse, and abandonment. And they were struggling with how such bad things could happen in God's world. This struggle has been called by various names—"Theodicy", "The Problem of Evil", "The Dark Night of the Soul"[9], etc. I call it "Jobe Syndrome".[10] I got mad at God when I was 18. I didn't have a very good reason for it (I was angry over losing a girlfriend!). My wife had more reason to be angry at God. Listen to her story…

My Story by Jean Hausmann

My mother died when I was nine. I was one of eight children—the middle child. Mom's last three births were in the time of her life when she was battling breast cancer which then progressed into her lungs and throughout her body! Because she was with child, mom would not accept any type of chemo treatment that might cause harm to her babies. At the age of forty-one, mom died leaving an infant of three months and the rest of us, motherless. She was a woman of joy, gentle ways, and so much love for all of us. Her loss took me, a nine-year-old, into an anger stage of five years where I did not want anything to do with God. My spirituality began to circle around our Blessed Mother Mary as I constantly asked her to be my Mother.

One day, when I was a child of nine years old, I remember opening the church door which seemed so huge to me. But I was on a mission to talk to our Blessed Mother about my needs! I remember the sound of my shoes clicking on the marble floor as I proceeded down the center isle headed toward the statue of Mary. Nobody was in the church but Mary and me! "Ah", I wondered, "How could it be that Mary has just the two of us here in this holy place?" I knelt in front of her statue and began to pray, my hands folded in reverent prayer, and my face totally gazing upon her compassionate face. "Mary, as you well know, I don't have my mom anymore and I am so sad! I am asking that you take my Mom's place and you be my mom from this day on! I don't want to talk with your Son anymore because I really do not believe that He understands how terrible this is that He took my mom away from me and my family! So, I am not going to talk to Him anymore! I'll just talk to you! Could you just give me a sign by letting tears come from your eyes, right here and now? This would be our own miracle, just between you and me!" So, for a while, I gazed at her face believing that tears would come from the statue! That did not happen. But I can say with certainty that she placed warmth within my body and I knew that she said "yes" to my request. After a while, I stood up from the altar rail, and looked at her saying, "It's o.k. that you are not going to cry for me; maybe instead, I will cry for others who may be sad too!" This day alone in the church with Mary took me into a relationship with our blessed Mother that took preference to Jesus, her Son.

One day, when I was fourteen years old, in the eighth grade, our teacher invited a scientist into our class as a guest speaker. This one man, above all other good people in my life as a kid growing up, changed my entire thinking of God taking mom away from all of us! He began to explain to us students the effect of herbicides and pesticides upon the foods that we eat. He spoke of how planes would sweep a powder-like formula over fruit and vegetable fields, killing weeds and insects and worms that would damage our foods in the fields. "Ah," he said, "and then we get the perfect looking apple, so beautiful to the eye with no known defects, and without in depth washing of this fruit or vegetable, we eat it, and diseases, such as cancer, come about without warning! And how about preservatives that keep canned fruit and vegetables on our shelves for months at a time, and we do not notice what is in the liquid of these canned foods! That enters into our bodies too! A real big one that causes illness and often, death, is smoking! We are actually causing illness by the choices we make when we choose to take on the deadly habit of filling our lungs with smoke, and damaging our otherwise healthy lungs! Oh, what damage we do! And sometimes we die! What are we doing to ourselves and each other in this world of ours?"

I remember that day which took place over 60 years ago because that scientist, by the grace of God, released my anger and my blaming God for my mom's death! Mom was a smoker! I remember tears streaming down my eyes with an overwhelming sense of relief as my spirit of love came back into me for the God I had once loved, was now again found. Ah, such a gift to a fourteen-year-old young lady who now looks upon this world as defective and imperfect! Thanks be to God!

I love Jean's story. It is a model for my whole book—science can help us understand God's world—a world that includes so many terrible and painful things. Science can help us heal from Jobe Syndrome. It helped Jean and it helped me. See if it works for you.

This book is written especially for Jobe Syndrome sufferers. Jobe Syndrome attacks the emotions as well as the intellect. The emotional component is the primary one immediately after a crisis of grief, trauma or loss—the immediate need is for support from others—holding, listening and being present in all ways. And this need can last for months and years. The secondary need is for meaning, purpose and understanding—this is the intellectual part. This is the part that this book primarily addresses. Sometimes, the grief and trauma are so severe that something like Cognitive Behavioral Therapy (CBT) is required. CBT uses thought and reasoning to heal the pain of trauma, grief and loss and to change behavior for the better. But there is also a spiritual component to trauma, grief and loss. The spiritual component of Jobe Syndrome sometimes requires pastoral counseling following a protocol like the one presented in chapter one. A protocol is simply a set of steps in the counseling process directed toward healing the pain of grief, trauma and loss. These steps help the griever to find God's role and support and meaning and purpose in the traumatic event(s). Sometimes we can find no meaning. Sometimes we can never know why. But this book is an attempt to find meaning and purpose in a sometimes very confusing world. I have experienced the power of science to uncover meaning and purpose where there seems to be none. Science and Religion can work together to reveal the presence of God and meaning and purpose in the universe. So this book is good for the believer—it can strengthen your faith. It is good for the unbeliever—it can kindle a spark of faith in you. At the very least, it will show you how faith in God can be rational—and scientific.

It does help if the reader has an appreciation of science. Chapter one is good for everyone. And so is chapter three on Miracles. Non-philosophers may want to skip chapter two on Metaphysics and Physics. Non-science readers may want to skip chapters four, five, six and seven. These chapters attempt to summarize lots of new scientific material that points to the Supreme Intellect that created the universe—God. I have tried hard to understand, to summarize and to translate this abundance of scientific material into a readable form, but it still takes some science knowledge to appreciate it. Some readers may not appreciate this kind of material. All readers should appreciate chapter eight on Brother Pain, chapter nine on Sister Death and chapter 10 on the second death. The Epilogue is where God answers Jobe, summarizing the whole book and modernizing God's response to Jobe in the last chapters of the Biblical Book of Jobe. Everything God made was "very good" (Genesis 1). Evil does not come from God. Every truly evil event in history came from Satan, an alien fallen angel who wants to be God. He seduced the first humans to commit the "original sin" (Genesis 3) that began an epidemic of evil throughout the world. The central message of this book is—God exists and God cares. God suffers with us. God is the answer to our pain. God has overcome evil.

This book summarizes some of the best authors in the field of Science and Religion, including Fr. Robert Spitzer, SJ (*New Proofs for the Existence of God*), Dr. Stephen Meyer (*Signature in the Cell*), Dr. Francis Collins (*The Language of God*) and Fr. Teilhard de Chardin, SJ (*The Phenomenon of Man*). I also use Dr. Stephen Hawking's books (*A Brief History of Time* and *The Grand Design*) as evidence for God in spite of his atheism. These authors reveal 4 contemporary scientific "proofs" for the existence of God: the argument from Anthropy, the argument from Entropy, the argument from DNA and the argument from Altruism. These arguments are modern enhancements to St. Thomas Aquinas' fifth proof for the existence of God, his "Teleological argument".

This book is intended to provide a great tool for the evangelization of people in the "Court of the Gentiles", science majors in particular and college students in general. My hope is to take my book to every college campus for presentation and book signing events to provide opportunities to evangelize the "nones" (people with no religion). At the Notre Dame Conference on "Cultures of Formation" (March 6, 2018), Bishop Robert Barren noted the increase in the number of young people identifying themselves as "nones". And he cited a Pew Research finding that the number one reason why millennials are rejecting religion is science—they believe they need to choose between belief in science and belief in religion.[11] This book demonstrates that this choice is a false dilemma—science and religion are approaching the same Truth that there is a Supreme Intelligence Who designed and created the universe and that this Being is also Benevolent.

CHAPTER ONE

Jobe Syndrome—When God Cries

"Jesus began to weep." (John 11: 35)

My career in spiritual care at Holy Cross Children's Services[12] has been as stimulating for my own growth as it has hopefully been for the young people and co-workers I have served during my 30 years there. Consider the case of Mandy[13], for example. Mandy was a 15-year-old girl who had recently entered one of our girls' residences. I was interviewing Mandy to demonstrate to our new Chaplain-intern, Rita, how to do a spiritual assessment with a new youth. This is one of our routine jobs as chaplain. (A chaplain is the staff person that is a specialist providing spiritual support to the clients; a chaplain-intern is someone aspiring to be a chaplain and is being coached and supervised by a chaplain.) The goal of spiritual assessment is to discover spiritual strengths and distress in their life stories. The three of us were huddled together in a small room near the chapel. Mandy had completed our written survey of questions about her spiritual history, beliefs, values and practices. I had reviewed her responses on the survey and was asking her to go into greater depth on some of the responses I highlighted as significant. I focused intently on Mandy as we got to the questions about spiritual distress. Rita was watching us and listening...

(Me):"Mandy, question 17 asked you if you ever wondered where God was when bad things happened to you. You said you "strongly agree". Can you tell me more about that?"

(Mandy):"Yeah. I was sexually abused by my dad. It started when I was 10 and it didn't stop till I was 13. That's when I told my teacher and she turned dad in to the police."

(Me):"Mandy, that must have been awful!

(Mandy):"It was. And that's why I can't understand it! **Where was God when I was raped? Why didn't God do something?"**

(We paused for a few moments of tense silence. I was so moved by her question that I diverted the session from my usual assessment mode. Normally, assessment is focused on the chaplain doing the active listening and the youth doing the talking—teaching the chaplain about her spirituality. The counseling comes in later sessions. But this time I was shocked into offering a response. What could I say to Mandy?)

(Me:)Mandy, would you like to know what I believe about what God was doing when you were raped?"

(Mandy:)"Yes."

(Me:) "I believe that God was crying."

(We paused again for a few silent moments.)

(Mandy:)"I never thought that God could cry..."

I believe this one thought opened up new possibilities for her relationship with God. I never did work with Mandy again, but Rita did and later confided in me that tears came to her own eyes at that moment in our session with Mandy—not for Mandy, but for herself: Rita had been raped as a teenager and had wondered about God, just like Mandy did— and the thought of God crying tears—over her having been raped— gave her a new sense of closeness to God. She was moved to tears. And I treasure her sharing that with me.

The Holy Cross ministry, like the hospital ministry, is one which is dealing with *crisis* in the life of the client and the client's family. They are in a grief process in many ways; they are faced with actual or potential major losses: life, freedom, self-respect, divorce, family split, etc. Many of our clients have suffered all kinds of abuse for many years and/or abandonment by the parent(s). Their lives are in crisis and they are taken away from whatever family they have and institutionalized. They believe life is not fair—God is not fair. "Why is all this happening to me? to my family? "God doesn't care". "God doesn't answer (my) prayer". "Where was God?" The client is experiencing Jobe Syndrome.

Jobe Syndrome Spectrum

Jobe Syndrome symptoms range from *disappointment with God* to *anger with God* to *agnosticism* (a state of doubt whether God is real or not) to *atheism* (a state of denial that God exists) to *Satanism* (belief that Satan—the personification of evil—rules the world). These symptoms can be ordered in the form of a spectrum ranging from alienation from God to outright antagonism. The Biblical book of Jobe addresses this spectrum. The patience of Jobe in the death of his children is legendary: He said,

> "Naked I came forth from my mother's womb,
> and naked shall I go back there.
> The LORD gave and the LORD has taken away;
> blessed be the name of the LORD!"
> [22] In all this Job did not sin, nor did he charge
> God with wrong. (Job 1:21-22)

But Jobe's patience ended in chapter 2. Chapter 3 begins with Jobe's despair:

> [3] Perish the day on which I was born, the night
> when they said, "The child is a boy!" (Job 3:3)

And Job went on to question God and argue against his religious friends during the next 34 chapters.

Disappointment With God is the title of an excellent book on this topic by Philip Yancey.[14] The subtitle, "Three Questions No One Asks Aloud" are three key questions that Jobe asks: "Is God unfair?" "Is God silent?" "Is God hidden?"[15] Jobe answers "yes" to each of them. "I am innocent, but God denies me justice." (Job 34:5; cf. 27:2). Rabbi Harold Kushner[16] summarizes the dilemma of Jobe Syndrome well: the key to the Book of Jobe is a forced choice among three propositions:

- God is all- powerful...
- God is just and fair...

- Jobe is a good person[17]

We would like to believe that all three are true, but because of Jobe's situation, Kushner claims that only two of the three can be true. One must be false. Jobe's friends claim that the third is false (Jobe is not a good person; otherwise he would not be experiencing the punishment of God Who is just). Jobe claims that number two is false (God is not just and fair). But Kushner claims that the fault is with the first proposition: (God is not almighty).[18] But Rabbi Kushner makes the solution overly simple—he eliminates the mystery in the problem of evil. On the other hand, Cardinal Robert Sarah respects the "incomprehensible" mystery of evil and he does not over-simplify:

> Evil raises an immense question, an enigma that is impossible to resolve. No one in any era of human history has succeeded in giving a satisfying response to the problem of evil.[19]

Cardinal Sarah refers to a Jewish philosopher, Hans Jonas, who also over-simplifies the problem of evil:

> In order for the goodness of God to be compatible with the existence of evil, he must not be almighty. More exactly, it is necessary for this God to have renounced power. In the simple fact of allowing human freedom lies a renunciation of power.[20]

His last statement is true—God gave up His control over human decisions, "a renunciation of power". But this does not mean that God is not almighty. God is in control of the universe in spite of humans (or angels) who reject His will. Sooner or later, love will conquer evil.

> But if God is not all powerful, then he is not God. He is the Almighty, but, at the same time, he wants to permit man to be truly free. Because the omnipotence of God is the omnipotence of love...[21]

"God is Love" (1 John 4:16) and Love is omnipotent—he will have his way in the end. And Love cannot contradict itself—love cannot be forced into someone's heart. Once God made humans, God permitted them to reject God's plan for the world; in other words, God's creation of humans with free will permitted people to "sin" (as well as to love).

> God does not will evil.[22] Christians know that God does not will evil. And if this evil exists, God is the first victim of it.[23]

> God is in no way, directly or indirectly, the cause of moral evil. He permits it, however, because he respects the freedom of his creatures, and, mysteriously, knows how to derive good from it.[24]

God is "mysteriously" able to accomplish good in spite of peoples' evil choices. God always has a "Plan B" when people reject his "Plan A". God always tries to get people to choose his will, to stop sin—God prods their consciences to follow his will. But evil perpetrators can reject the voice of conscience and commit terrible crimes against innocent victims. But the unrepentant and unapologetic perpetrator will experience everlasting torture of conscience and separation from God and God's people in hell. The rapist can choose to rape in spite of the above. God *won't* take back God's gift of free will. And our Holy Cross youths (and families, and others) will continue to wonder: "Where was God when I was raped?" The actual prayers ("letters to God") of some Holy Cross youths offer many examples of the religious thinking involved in Jobe Syndrome:

> Dear God,
>
> I don't believe in You because every time I ask You to do something it seems like it don't never happen. And another thing, if You was so real You wouldn't have let that happen to my mother and plus I be asking You to show me something that you know that my mother is doing all right. It don't never happen.[25]

This youth doesn't think that God is fair. Can you blame him? God doesn't seem to be answering his prayers... His mom is in big trouble and he can't even find out how she's doing... Why doesn't God let him know?

Here is someone else's complaint...

> "As God lives who takes away my right,
>   the Almighty, who has made my life bitter,
>   [3] So long as I still have life breath in me,
>   the breath of God in my nostrils,
>   [4] My lips shall not speak falsehood,

> nor my tongue utter deceit!
> ⁵ Far be it from me to account you right;
> till I die I will not renounce my innocence.

This quote is from Jobe (27:2-5). It is a more formal way of stating the same kind of issues as those in the Holy Cross letter(s). Jobe sounds like a Holy Cross youth.

Ken Pargament *et al.* have demonstrated a connection between anger at God and poor mental health.[26] It is a condition that needs treatment. At Holy Cross, we have developed a pastoral counseling protocol for treating Jobe Syndrome.[27] Part of the healing of Jobe Syndrome can come from understanding the concept of free will. With this understanding, the victim can experience God's presence in the rape as shouting to the perpetrator "Don't do this! Don't hurt my child!" and after he disobeys *God's will*, then God is weeping (John 11:35) and lamenting through tears, "Why, why did you do this to my child?" For the youth or family member to know and believe that God wept when they were raped can help them to heal from Jobe Syndrome. For the youth or family member to know that God is sorry that the rape happened (like the time of Noah when God was sorry that he made humans: Gen. 6:6)— this can be comforting to the victim. God would like to say, "I'm so sorry that my creature(s) did this to you/ to your family (Jeremiah 42:10)."[28] For the youth to know that even Jesus felt abandoned by God:

> And at three o'clock Jesus cried out in a loud voice, "*Eloi, Eloi, lema sabachthani?*" which is translated, "My God, my God, why have you forsaken me?" (Mark 15:34—Psalm 22)

For us to know that Jesus' prayer—"Abba, Father," he said, "everything is possible for you. Take this cup from me." (Mark 14:36)–God answered with a "no"—God did not take away the cup. These verses of scripture can help heal Jobe Syndrome. To know that there are at least "Eleven reasons why people aren't healed"[29] helps youths to understand they're not the only ones whose prayers don't seem to be answered and there are often reasons for God to answer "no". "Some of God's greatest gifts are unanswered prayers."[30] To know that pain, suffering, sickness and even death can have a meaning and purpose in one's life[31] can help heal Jobe Syndrome. These are many of the balms for healing one's heart and mind.

Perhaps as important as the answers to Jobe's questions are, it may be even more important to experience a *catharsis* (a release of emotions) by expressing one's anger with God and to experience that this expression is O.K. with God[32]. Jobe's key questions were not answered by God; e.g., God never refuted Jobe's claim that God was not fair (Job 38-42). Rather, Jobe's anger and confrontation of God are affirmed by God while the "friends" of Jobe (who defended God) are rebuked: "you have not spoken of me what is right, as my servant Jobe has" (Job 42:7). God declares Jobe's anger and confrontation as having been "what is right". What a surprise for us conventional believers! It's O.K. to be angry with God! This, too, can help to heal Jobe Syndrome. But the healing process can be enhanced when this knowledge is actually acted upon and the victim vents his/her anger at God.[33] This is the kind of prayer that can be found in the Psalms, particularly those with the lament themes: e.g., Psalms 22, 44, 88 and 109.[34] This catharsis of anger in prayer may do more for the healing process than all the explanations mentioned above. This experience can be enhanced by having the grieving person compose and pray their own psalm of lament. This intervention was used by Chaplain Joe Martinus at Holy Cross Services. He used this technique in the case of Corey.

Corey's Story[35]

Corey was sexually abused at the age of 5 by a 17-year-old male babysitter. This abuse went on for nearly one year. Criminal sexual conduct (CSC) charges were pressed and the perpetrator was prosecuted. Corey reported being afraid of this man and worried that he will harm her again. Corey was a very angry, aggressive, 14-year-old child. She was combative toward her mother; the mother was afraid of her. Corey was hospitalized at 9 years of age after she threatened her brother with a knife. At 12 years of age, she was hospitalized in a psychiatric program for 10 days as the result of a suicidal gesture. Corey has been diagnosed with epilepsy as well as a severe psychological disorder – a florid psychotic process that may include social withdrawal, personality decompensation, disordered affect, as well as erratic, sometimes aggressive behaviors. She was in several treatment programs and foster homes before placement at St. Vincent Home in Saginaw, Michigan. She was charged with criminal sexual conduct against two younger, female children. When Chaplain Joe Martinus questioned Corey concerning the reason for her placement at St. Vincent Home, she was evasive, embarrassed; not wanting him to know…

Corey's biological parents had been divorced since she was 3 years of age. Her mother had been remarried and divorced. The mother was living with a significant other. She had a reported history of alcohol abuse, depression, and a suicide attempt. She was cited for neglect (leaving Corey home alone) in the spring of that year. Corey's father lived in Arizona. She described him as a "drug addict and alcoholic." She has had no contact with him for several years. She had a 15-year-old stepbrother who appeared to be favored over Corey by the mother.

Corey stated that she believed in God. She attributed her belief to "belonging to church so long", as well as her experience of answered prayer. She expressed a negative view of God – angry, vengeful, and punitive. Corey was uncertain of God's love for her as well as God's willingness to forgive her sins. She has expressed interest in learning more about God. Corey was in the practice of daily and nightly prayer. She identified with the Christian/Protestant tradition. She had been involved with the Baptist faith and more recently with the Salvation Army. Corey had never been baptized. She had accepted Christ as her Savior numerous times. As a result of her responses on the assessment instrument and during the interview process, two issues were noted for immediate attention.

- a shame based view of herself (low self-esteem).
- a conflicted relationship with God (a negative image of God)

Altogether, Joe spent over 17 hours in individual pastoral counseling with Corey during her 16 months in treatment at

St. Vincent Home. About ten hours were devoted specifically to implementing the Jobe Syndrome treatment plan as outlined above (see appendix B, p. 221).

When Joe asked Corey to list her "spiritual pains", she included her parents' divorce, her parents' alcoholism and drug abuse, abandonment by her father, her being a victim of sexual abuse and her being a perpetrator of sexual abuse. When Joe asked Corey to describe God, she used words like "mean", "angry", "hurtful", "devilish". When Joe asked her to draw a picture of God, she produced Image 2:

Image 2:

Joe proceeded with Objectives 3 and 4 of the plan: Identifying Biblical support for expressing her conflict with God and praying the anger psalms with Joe. Then Joe asked Corey to compose her own psalm / poem:

"A prayer for the angry!"

"Please Lord forgive my sins-I'm feeling angry a lot lately and cannot seem to control it anymore. I need your help and don't know why I'm angry. Can you please tell me why I get so angry for no reason?"

"Worries:"

"God, I'm feeling alone.
I been wishing that I was gone.
It feels like I'm down with Satan in the pit.
God, you are the one that knows me well.
You know things that are going to happen.
Why won't you tell me so I can be aware?
I'm just sitting here feeling hot in this chair.
God could you help me with my stress and anger?
You're the one I can turn to.
You're the one that can help me out.
Forgive my sins, God,
For I still have a life to live."

After several sessions and several months addressing her image of God, Joe asked Corey to draw another picture of God. Her new picture of God is Image 3:

Image 3:

From Corey's participation in the prayer-ritual and from Image 3, Joe could evaluate that his interventions helped Corey to image God differently. We believe God's Spirit was intervening with Corey. The change in her tone can be seen in Corey's artwork. Figure one was chaotic and agitated, a lightning bolt penetrated the soul/center, lines crossed over each other, etc. Figure two conveys the aura of peace, the Spirit/dove in the center, the pastel colors less shocking than those in figure one. Corey pictures a calmer Spirit inside. And her calmer Spirit showed in her behavior as well. Earlier in her placement, Corey feared she might be "escalated" from this medium-secure St. Vincent Home to a maximum secure program, because of her anger being out of control. But by the end of her 16 months, she was finishing the program with a recommendation for release.

For the pastoral counselor, the role of empathetic listening[36] is more important than the role of teaching new understandings of God. Remember the "friends" of Job who *began* with quality pastoral care:

When they saw [Jobe] from a distance, they could hardly recognize him; they began to weep aloud, and they tore their robes and sprinkled dust on their heads. Then they sat on the ground with him for seven days and seven nights. No one said a word to him, because they saw how great his suffering was. (Job 2: 12f)

The presence and empathy from Jobe's friends was very helpful to Jobe. But they got into trouble as soon as they opened their mouth to defend God (Job 4). Their defense of God only aggravated the anger and pain of Jobe. And God rebuked the friends for their poor "pastoral counseling" (Job 42:7). Once they started with their "premature proclamations" of God's goodness and "instant solutions" to the complexities of Jobe Syndrome, they became "absent" to Jobe (unsupportive) rather than "present".[37] And presence is perhaps the most important intervention of all.

The chaplain / religious minister can represent God to a grieving person. The grieving person can experience God's presence in the presence of the religious minister. The caring attitude of God's representative can be a healing intervention all by itself. Much of Chaplain Joe Martinus' time with Corey was spent in active listening and presence. Perhaps this was the key to Corey's healing from Jobe Syndrome.

CHAPTER TWO

Physics, Metaphysics, Statistics and the Scientific Method

(Note to the reader: This chapter attempts to translate concepts of classical philosophy, philosophy of science and statistics into a readable form. If you get bogged down in terminology, please proceed to Chapter 3 on Miracles)

Modern Science has become a significant resource alongside Theology in the treatment of Jobe Syndrome. The whole spectrum of symptoms of Jobe Syndrome can be addressed by scientists. Image 4 is an outline of the spectrum.

Image 4:

Disappointment with God	Anger at God	Agnostic (Uncertain if God exists)	Atheist (Certain that God does not exist)	Satanist (God is evil)

Sometimes when Jobe Syndrome is not treated, it can progress through all five phases of the spectrum as stages, usually beginning with Disappointment with God:

- God let me down
- God didn't answer my prayer
- God took away my loved one
- God didn't stop my abuse

If these things happen, the emotion can change from disappointment to anger. Abusive happenings can lead the victim to doubt whether there can be a loving God. The victim can become an agnostic or an atheist. There is considerable evidence that the emotional issues like abuse and a problematical relationship with one's father (or the early death of a father) are very important influences toward atheism. Psychologist Paul Vitz referred to several quantitative studies in this regard and did his own research in the form of case studies of prominent atheists.[38] Emotional issues appear to be more important than intellectual ones for atheists. When severe abuse occurs, it becomes difficult to doubt that Satan is in control of the universe. The victim experiences a transition from no (benevolent) God to a diabolical god; the universe seems programmed to be abusive. The person who believes this has the most severe case of Jobe Syndrome.

How can science help a person with Jobe Syndrome?

Metaphysics and Physics

Metaphysics is as old as human evolution. It probably began when the first human encountered animals. It most likely began with the eyes—virtually every animal has those two eyes looking at me. Looking into the eyes of another being makes me think, "Now there is something out there that is looking at me just like I am looking at it. I wonder if they are thinking like I am thinking. Now that being is alive and conscious, just like me. That being is different from the rocks. It must have a 'soul', a 'spirit', a 'self' that animates it. A spirit / self must be in it, just like my spirit / self is in me." Animism was born—the belief that spirits inhabit the bodies of animals and humans. And with the birth of animism came the birth of metaphysics—there is something real that is invisible and non-physical that animates bodies. Eventually, animism evolved into monotheism—the belief that there is some ultimate invisible reality that animates the universe.[39] Likewise, animism eventually evolved into humanism—the belief that humans have a spirit that is qualitatively superior to other animals—capable of inventing / discovering technology and ethics. Metaphysics expanded to at least three levels— animal souls, human souls, and the soul of the universe: God. All of these souls or spirits are invisible, but we can tell that they exist by the animation of their bodies. When the soul / spirit departs, there is the same complex conglomeration of chemicals in the body, but no animation—death happens. There is evidence for metaphysical realities.

Scientists strive for objectivity. Many do not like accounting for human consciousness. They do not like dealing with the "Mind-Body Problem".[40] Modern science thrived on the outdated notion that everything in the universe could be explained as bunches of atoms that behaved like tiny billiard balls. The mind was nothing but a brain—a part of the body. However, contemporary science has become more metaphysical—physics has discovered metaphysics. Newtonian Physics was one of the greatest scientific revolutions[41] that transformed the concept of the universe from a more primitive atomic view to a more sophisticated one that added the gravitational field to the atoms—from a "billiard-ball" universe of atoms banging into each other, to one with atoms being attracted to each other by the force of gravity. The gravitational field is invisible, but we know it exists because of its visible and measurable effects on objects. Not that we can see atoms—they are invisible even to most microscopes—but we can see large bundles of atoms as objects in our universe, and we can observe the effects of gravity, for example, on the moon in relation to the earth. And Newton measured the force of gravity between objects and the gravitational constant using Newton's Law.[42] The gravitational field is invisible, measured only by its effects. A skeptic might say, "If I can't see it, I don't believe it." That is what the atheist says about God. But scientists believe in many things that can't be seen—and the number of these things is speedily growing. It could be said that physics is expanding into the realm of metaphysics; there are more and more realities in the universe that are invisible and non-physical—metaphysical.

Science has evolved from a worldview where the only reality was matter (bundles of atoms) to a worldview that questions whether or not there is such a thing as matter (matter may be totally composed of force fields and waves rather than matter).[43] We have evolved in our thinking that "everything in the universe is nothing but a bundle of atoms" to the most current view that all of what we see and touch as objects in our universe are mostly composed of empty space—what we feel as a solid object is actually very tiny electrons flying around the tiny atomic nucleus with lots of empty space in between. We used to think of atoms as the smallest particles in the universe, but about 100 years ago, scientists discovered that atoms are made up of protons, neutrons and electrons.[44] The atomic mass of a proton or a neutron is defined as one atomic weight unit[45]; the mass of an electron is virtually zero.[46] We never touch the protons or neutrons—we "feel" the speeding electrons flying around the nucleus of protons and neutrons even though electrons are so small that they are virtually weightless. Then in 1964 two physicists invented "quarks"—particles that make up protons and neutrons but "there was little evidence for their physical existence until deep inelastic scattering experiments at the Stanford Linear Accelerator Center in 1968".[47] The atom smashing experiments provided evidence that the quark-theory was true. The quarks help explain the electromagnetic fields and forces in the subatomic particles and the new discovery of the strong and weak fields and forces in the nucleus of the atom.

The discovery of the strong and weak force fields in the nucleus of the atom had not yet occurred when I was studying chemistry in 1966. I was in the Introduction to College Chemistry course with the legendary professor Emil T. Hoffman and 400 fellow freshmen at Notre Dame. We had no textbook—Emil T. Hoffman was in the process of writing his own and we received his entire manuscript in the form of weekly handouts and lectures. So we studied the structure of the atom. We learned that the previously accepted theory of atom came from Niels Bohr—an atom with a central nucleus of protons and neutrons surrounded by electrons in various circular or elliptical orbits. Dr. Hoffman described how the newer discovery of the Heisenburg uncertainty principle and quantum mechanics had changed the concept of the atom to include a cloud of probable electron locations in place of the smooth orbits of the Bohr model. Yet in all the confusion of learning about the atom, I never heard anyone ask the question: "Opposite forces attract each other. Like forces repel each other. How do the positive charged protons stay together in the nucleus of the atom? Why don't they repel each other?" Now we know that the answer is the strong nuclear force—"the strong nuclear force holds most ordinary matter together…" [48] Even Dr. Hoffman had not yet learned about the strong nuclear force field in 1966—it was in the process of being invented at the time. The strong nuclear force field—like the gravitational force field—is invisible, non-material and therefore metaphysical—physics has again crossed over the horizon of the material world and into the non-material world of metaphysics.

Many scientists would protest: "The force fields are not metaphysics. They are part of matter, and therefore part of physics. As such they are measurable, testable and predictable. Metaphysics is not measurable, testable, and predictable." Aha! Now we are begging the question of what is science and what is the scientific method?

The Scientific Method

There are many ways to define the scientific method. Wikipedia defines the scientific method as "a method of procedure that has characterized natural science since the 17th century, consisting in systematic observation, measurement, and experiment, and the formulation, testing and modification of hypotheses."[49] Many would say that this definition of the scientific method disqualifies metaphysics from being considered "scientific". You can't "observe" the "spirit", the "soul" or God (key concepts in traditional metaphysics). You can't "measure" these things. You can't design "experiments" on them. This suggests to me that one could define science as the attempt to explain reality without appealing to God— as if God didn't exist. At least this may be part of the origin of the scientific method.[50] Let's see what we can discover about the universe without jumping to the conclusion that "God made it the way it is". Let's explain how the universe came to be without using the Bible creation story. Of course, many scientists eventually went from explaining the universe **as if** God does not exist to "God does not exist". This latter development of science reached its peak in the 19th century with the advent of Darwinian evolution, Marxist Communism and Freudian psychology—creation without a creator, government without religion, and psychology without a soul. Prior to these famous atheists, most scientists were religious—some were even priests and monks (e.g., Copernicus, Roger Bacon, Gregor Mendel). Johannes Kepler wanted to be a minister but was never ordained. "Kepler described his new astronomy as 'an excursion into Aristotle's Metaphysics'".[51]

In the 20th century, there were two great priest-scientists who countered the trend toward atheistic science. Father Teilhard de Chardin was a Jesuit priest, a paleontologist and geologist who offered one of the first theistic theories of evolution.[52] The second was Father Georges Lemaitre. He…

> "proposed the theory of the expansion of the universe, widely misattributed to Edwin Hubble. He was the first to derive what is now known as

Hubble's law and made the first estimation of
what is now called the Hubble constant, which
he published in 1927, two years before Hubble's
article. Lemaitre also proposed what became
known as the Big Bang theory of the origin of
the universe...[53]

When empirical evidence began to support the Big Bang
theory, the world of science was in shock. The universe has
a beginning. An unbelievable concept! Atheists religiously
avoided the concept of the beginning of the universe—it
sounded too much like the Bible. [54] The universe had no
beginning and no end. It was made up of matter alone—and
the matter in the universe always was and always will be.
Atheists claimed no faith and no metaphysics. Science had
to do with matter and the scientific method producing verifi-
able and testable theories, not metaphysics. Prior to 1927, the
argument over the eternal universe vs. the origin of the universe was a matter of faith—atheists believed in the eternal
universe and religious people believed in a created universe.
Neither side had any empirical data for their faith-claim—and
neither side expected that there would ever be any empirical data. How can one find any evidence about an event that
happened millions of years ago? Each side had a position that
could be considered metaphysics rather than physics. And
neither side expected that their faith-claim would ever be
confirmed or refuted.

But then came the measurement of the "red-shift".[55] Stars,
planets and galaxies were measured by their velocities
as moving away from the center of the universe—the Big
Bang proposed by Father Georges Lemaitre—unbelievable

evidence for faith in the universe that is not eternal, that has a beginning. This was a scandalous concept for many scientists. "How could there be a beginning in time for the universe? Scientific evidence for the Big Bang refuted the atheist concept of the eternal universe. Perhaps the greatest contemporary mind in the science world was the late Stephen Hawking of Cambridge University, famous for his work on Black Holes. He has spent much of his career in quest of *The Grand Design*[56], the grand theory that would combine Einstein's General Theory of Relativity and quantum mechanics[57] and re-establish the eternal universe theory. In his book, *A Brief History of Time—From the Big Bang to Black Holes* (1988), Hawking predicted that the "Grand Theory" combining General Relativity theory and Quantum Mechanics would be discovered in his lifetime. In his book, *The Grand Design* (2010) he claimed that the Grand Theory was more or less achieved. However, by the standards he set in the former book, the Grand Theory continues to remain elusive.

Entropy and Natural Selection

In *A Brief History of Time*, atheist physicist Stephen Hawking acknowledged the evidence for the Big Bang—it's in his subtitle.[58] In his earlier research he had "proved" that the Big Bang exploded from a "singularity", a "black hole" in which all the matter of the universe was condensed into a single point—and the laws of physics did not apply to anything prior to it. But in his book, *The Grand Design*, Hawking's goal was to outline the possibility of the Grand Theory and predicted the components of it. The Grand Theory would eliminate the Big Bang. But Hawking also acknowledged the 2nd law of thermodynamics. The 2nd law of thermodynamics is a law, not a

theory, and on the surface, it is a scandal to the evolution theorists—it seems to deny the possibility of the spontaneous
origin of living cells from chemicals and to deny the possibility
of the complex structures of the higher animals and human
bodies and brains to be the product of natural selection alone.
Natural Selection is the key to evolution theory. It is more
commonly known as "the survival of the fittest."[59] The mutations that accidentally occur in the reproduction of living cells
can enable the new organism to be a stronger one than its
parent, giving it more survival potential in the competition
for life. Higher forms of life evolve from lower forms of life.
Evolution depends upon the concept of natural selection.

The Second Law of Thermodynamics can be stated as a law
predicting that—sooner or later—all order and complexity
in the universe will break down—all natural processes proceed in the direction toward chaos. In fact, the second law
names the measure of chaos—it is called "Entropy". So the
2nd law is often stated in the form: "all natural events spontaneously proceed toward increased Entropy (increased
chaos)". Entropy is a mathematical version of the common
sense phenomenon that everything tends to break down—
energy and maintenance are always needed to repair or prevent breakdowns. However, evolution theory (by means of
natural selection) attempts to explain how simple forms of life
could have evolved into complex forms of life—in other words,
how natural processes increase order and complexity (rather
than chaos) and how everything naturally organized rather
than broke down. Evolution theory and natural selection can
explain how lower forms of life evolved into higher forms of life.
However, natural selection seems to fail to explain how living
cells could spontaneously be animated from chemicals—how

life could have been "selected" as more "fit" than inanimate chemicals. Life is so delicate—it is not more "fit" than death— and in our universe, the rule is "survival of the fittest". The second law of thermodynamics defines "fitness" in the form of Entropy. And Entropy is defined as a measure of disorder/ chaos. A living cell is a masterpiece of order and complexity— millions of molecules "cooperating" in a state of equilibrium in constant motion in respiration, hydration, nutrition, repro- duction and waste elimination. A living cell should never have happened (according to the law of Entropy). It is too delicate to survive.

Atheists need to find some way to eliminate the claim of cre- ation of the first cell by a Creator. (Remember my definition of science as the process of explaining the universe without appealing to God.) So, the atheists appeal to two escape routes: first, they use the thermodynamic exception of the "open system" vs. the "closed system" to deny the relevance of thermodynamics in the discussion. Secondly, they criti- cize the theists for desperately defending the "God of the Gaps"—a concept that they claim to be outdated.

First, the thermodynamics: an "open system" is a situation in which the boundaries of the system are permeable—matter or energy can pass through them. For example, planet earth is an "open system"—constantly receiving enough solar energy to enable life (but not so much energy as to destroy life). In the case of an open system like planet earth, there can occur spontaneous events that produce a temporary increase in "order" or other imbalances of energy where Entropy tempo- rarily decreases rather than increases. These events seem to violate the 2nd Law of Thermodynamics and the inevitable increase in Entropy—but they don't. Eventually, the sun's fuel will be consumed, the sun and the earth will cool down toward absolute zero[60] and maximum Entropy of the solar system will occur (perhaps millions of years from now!). The possibility of temporary fluctuations in the direction of order and disorder, lower and higher values of Entropy in an open system, is a loophole for the atheists to use to explain how evolution can spontaneously produce huge increases in order and complexity of living things (and huge reductions in Entropy). The solar energy that comes to earth in the correct amount has fueled the evolution process and has enabled order to come from chaos, decreasing Entropy, temporarily. Eventually, Entropy will inevitably win and life will end on planet earth—but it will possibly take millions of years to happen. This loophole has enabled atheistic scientists to say that Entropy and the 2nd law do not prohibit evolution from proceeding in the direction of order and complexity—planet earth is an "open system".

However, the kind of complexity we find in a living cell is virtually impossible whether the system is an open or closed one.[61] Even in an open system where kinetic energy, heat energy, electrical energy or matter can enter or leave, complexity and order spontaneously decrease (and entropy increases). This obedience to the second law of thermodynamics is supported by common sense as well as mathematics. Science often uses models to illustrate concepts. Michael Behe used a mouse-trap.[62] Even a mechanism as simple as a mousetrap could not have assembled itself in gradual steps—it is "irreducibly complex". William Paley used a watch.[63] There is no way I can believe that the watch assembled itself. It is the product of intelligent design. I offer as a model a house of cards:

Image 5:

Image 5 shows the cards in the form of a one-story "house of cards". Common sense and the law of entropy would agree that the house of cards is an "ordered" or "designed" house—a low-entropy state of the system and a delicate, fragile equilibrium. Adding kinetic energy to this system in the form of shaking the box will, of course, collapse the house of cards instantly, producing an increase in entropy (disorder) and a random distribution of the cards. I say, "of course", because this is another case of the law of entropy agreeing with common sense. But what if I keep on shaking the box a million times—would one of those million shakes reproduce the house of cards? Common sense would say "no", but the laws of entropy and probability would say "possibly". It is possible that one shake in a million would reproduce the house of cards. The problem is, the very next shake would collapse it again. If it ever happened, it would only last for an instant.

This situation is problematic for the evolution of the first living cell. The first living cell requires delicate structures (like the house of cards) to not only "spontaneously" happen, but to happen many times—simultaneously. The nucleus, the mitochondria, the cell membrane, the ribosomes, etc., all need to evolve simultaneously—like several houses of cards and several stories in each house—in order to "assemble" a living cell.[64] And like the houses of cards, each part of the cell is a delicate structure, likely to crumble into pieces with the slightest application of heat energy or kinetic energy, before all the pieces can be captured by the cell wall, positioned in place, and function in sync with all the other delicate structures. This kind of complexity is extremely less probable than the assembly of many houses of cards—no matter whether the system is open or closed. Entropy dictates the most probable state of the system and the living cell system is extremely improbable.

Biologist Michael Behe tried to illustrate this by examining one particular organ—the bacterium flagellum—and discovering the "staggering complexity" of even such a "simple" organ—and the huge "difficulty of gradually putting the system together" in an evolutionary context.[65] Behe went on to claim that the living cell and "Life on earth at its most fundamental level, in its most critical components, is the product of intellectual activity."[66]

> There is an elephant in the roomful of scientists who are trying to explain the development of life. The elephant is labelled "intelligent design." To a person who does not feel obliged to restrict his search to unintelligent causes,

the straightforward conclusion is that many biochemical systems were designed. They were designed not by the laws of nature, not by chance and necessity; rather, they were *planned*. The designer knew what the systems would look like when they were completed, then took steps to bring the systems about.[67]

Behe claims that this discovery of intelligent design in nature

"...must be ranked as one of the greatest achievements in the history of science...the observation of the intelligent design of life is as momentous as the observation that the earth goes around the sun or that disease is caused by bacteria or that radiation is emitted in quanta... Why does the scientific community not greedily embrace its startling discovery? Why is the observation of design handled with intellectual gloves? The dilemma is that while one side of the elephant is labeled intelligent design, the other side might be labeled God.[68]

As we reach the end of this book, we are left with no substantive defense against what feels to be a strange conclusion: that life was designed by an intelligent agent.[69]

Darwin's Black Box was originally published in 1996. It was reprinted in 2006. In his "Afterword" to the latter printing, Behe wrote

... a decade after the publication of *Darwin's Black Box* the scientific argument for design is stronger than ever... the book's argument for design stands."[70]

The conclusion that something was designed can be made quite independently of knowledge of the designer. As a matter of procedure, the design must first be apprehended before there can be any further question about the designer. The inference to design can be held with all the firmness that is possible in this world, without knowing anything about the designer.[71]

And Behe is not a creationist. He is a biologist and he is religious.[72] But he does not interpret Genesis literally.

Many people think that questioning Darwinian evolution must be equivalent to espousing creationism. As commonly understood, creationism involves belief in an earth formed about ten thousand years ago, an interpretation of the Bible that is still very popular. For the record, I have no reason to doubt that the universe is the billions of years old that physicists say it is. Further, I find the idea of common descent (that all organisms share a common ancestor) fairly convincing, and have no particular reason to doubt it... Although Darwin's mechanism—natural selection working on variation—might explain many things, however, I do not believe it explains molecular life.[73]

The lack of evidence for molecular evolution remains one of those gaps in Darwin's theory that just won't go away. Behe quotes one of his colleagues, Klaus Dose:

> More than 30 years of experimentation on the origin of life in the fields of chemical and molecular evolution have led to a better perception of the immensity of the problem of the origin of life on Earth rather than to its solution. At present all discussion on principal theories and experiments in the field either end in stalemate or in a confession of ignorance.[74]

Behe describes all the biochemicals that have been synthesized in the lab over those 30 years—and most of the building blocks of life have been chemically synthesized in the lab—including proteins and nucleic acids and pieces of DNA. But even with amazing advances in the lab synthesis of biochemicals, the problem gets clearer in focus.

> Most readers will quickly see the problem. There were no chemists four billion years ago. Neither were there any chemical supply houses, distillation flasks, nor any of the many other devices that the modern chemist uses daily in his or her lab… the involvement of some intelligence is unavoidable.[75]

Two other colleagues of Behe, Gerald Joyce and Leslie Orgel, call the molecular evolution of RNA a "near miracle":

Scientists interested in the origins of life seem to divide neatly into two classes. The first… believe that RNA must have been the first replicating molecule and that chemists are exaggerating the difficulties of nucleotide synthesis…The second group of scientists are much more pessimistic. They believe that the de novo appearance of oligonucleotides on the primitive earth would have been a near miracle… Time will tell which is correct.[76]

God of the Gaps

The second way that the atheists attempt to stop the discussion about God is by denying the relevance of the "God of the Gaps" discussion.[77] "God of the Gaps" is a derogatory name for the God of the theists who have always claimed that the existence of God is needed to explain certain things—like creation, for example. Atheists review the history of science to show how many formerly unexplainable things have been explained by the scientific method. And the number of explanations of things by science is accelerating. And there are so few things left unexplained that most scientists believe that it won't be long before everything is explained (by means of Hawking's "Grand Theory of Everything"?). There are very few "gaps" left in our scientific explanation of things. (The evolution of a single living cell is one of those gaps.) Atheists claim that those of us who focus on one gap in our scientific knowledge to prove that God exists are desperately clinging to a branch of the tree that is being sawed off—we are going to be embarrassed, sooner or later. "Grow up and stop holding on to the gaps in scientific knowledge!" they say. Even theistic scientist Francis Collins believes that we should not use the God-of-the-Gaps argument.[78]

Some theists are not intimidated by the "God of the Gaps" and the "open system" claims. In fact, both of these are metaphysical claims and matters of "faith" rather than science — after more than a century of failed attempts to duplicate the creation of the first living cell in the lab, it remains a huge gap in scientific knowledge.[79] It lingers in a metaphysical realm of faith—a faith that predicts there will be a physical explanation rather than a metaphysical one. That is the faith of the atheist. Faith is also required for the "open system" claim. Our current data suggests that our universe (not our planet earth) is a "closed system" rather than an "open system"—all the galaxies in the universe came from the Black Hole prior to the Big Bang, meaning that all matter and energy in the universe was condensed in that Black Hole and after the Big Bang, all matter and energy in the universe continued to have a boundary, albeit a rapidly expanding boundary. No matter or energy is being added to or subtracted from the expanding universe. The evidence points to a universe that is a closed system rather than an open one—and therefore the law of Entropy increase does apply to it. It is a metaphysical claim for the atheist to say that the universe is an open system—it is their belief and their hope that a new Grand Theory will produce empirical evidence for it. At this time there is no empirical evidence for either theory.

Stephen Hawking did not deny the apparent contradiction of the law of Entropy in our universe. In fact, he acknowledged what he called the thermodynamic "arrow" that inexorably pushes the universe toward disorder and chaos.[80] His method of avoiding the Big Bang beginning of the universe and the contradiction between evolution toward order and the inevitable increase in Entropy (disorder) was to postulate multi-universes[81], including one prior to the Black Hole and the Big Bang where the "arrow" of Entropy was reversed and everything in the universe naturally moved into order and complexity and intelligent life was impossible.[82] In fact, the multi-universe theory enabled Hawking to claim that all physical laws could be totally different in other universes. This is a statement of faith rather than a scientific statement—this is another case of metaphysics where there is apparently no possibility of observing or verifying the existence of another universe. In *The Grand Theory,* Hawking admits that a single Grand Theory of everything may be impossible.[83]

Aliens

Stephen Hawking has made another faith statement in a documentary called "Into the Universe with Stephen Hawking"— he believes in the existence of intelligent aliens.[84] This is consistent with his claim that there are multiple universes— multiverses increase the number of potentially habitable planets and therefore the possibility of alien life forms. But I would suggest that belief in intelligent aliens is equivalent to believing in "gods" and in hostile "gods"—they may be more intelligent (and powerful) than we are—that's why planet earth is at risk, according to Hawking. These alien "gods" could destroy us. I would suggest that Hawking is perhaps not an "atheist" after all—he sounds more like a polytheist, believing in many gods of varying intelligence and power and hostility. It sounds like Greek mythology where many gods behave badly. Is not the belief that there is a most Intelligent

Designer who ordered the universe in a benevolent way—a God above all gods—more believable than the polytheism of Hawking? The Being with the highest intelligence (and benevolence) is comparable to what theists call God.

Monotheists believe in one God above all other gods who is in control of the entire universe. I suggest that Hawking's faith in aliens is not as reasonable as the monotheist's faith in God. Christians also have a kind of belief in aliens. Christians believe in angels and fallen angels (demons). Angels and Demons are not humans and so they could also be called aliens. Stephen Hawking may not be as far from Theism as he appears.

New Proofs for God[85]

We will be exploring the boundaries between physics and metaphysics and between chemicals and cells in this book. These boundaries are apparently becoming more permeable than ever in our history as physics has entered the invisible world of particles smaller than the atom and the proton, and "quarks" and electrons that act more like oscillating fields of energy than particles. Indeed, the discovery of the four fundamental forces of nature (gravity, electromagnetism, nuclear strong force and the nuclear weak force)[86] are dependent on non-material, invisible force fields that blur the boundary between physics and metaphysics. The animation of the first living cell from a "primordial soup"[87] of chemicals continues to elude a physical explanation and continues to beg for a metaphysical one. Even a brilliant atheist-scientist like Stephen Hawking admits that the "anthropic principle"[88]— the apparent design in the universe that seems to have ordered the universe to produce and nurture life—seems to point to God (even though he is attempting to explain it without God). Our excursion from physics to metaphysics will show that the evidence for faith in God is stronger than ever. Indeed, we have several "new proofs for God"[89] that we did not have prior to the 20th century. The God-of-the-Gaps is alive and well.

Statistics and Probability

Theists believe God is in control of the universe. But it doesn't feel like that at times. It often seems like events are random and chaotic. Some events that look like accidents are not actually accidents. They are "controlled" by statistics and probability. Of course, the atheists believe that everything is an accident—nothing has purpose or design. Many theists believe that there is no such thing as an accident. They say "there is always a reason why something happened". Albert Einstein is credited with the statement, "God doesn't play dice".[90] However, quantum mechanics has discovered that the atom itself is governed by chance, statistics and probability. Erwin Schrodinger's equations changed the world of nuclear physics by calculating the probability of the electron being in a certain quantum state around the nucleus of the atom.[91] We can only calculate a probable position of the electron because of Heisenburg's uncertainty principle—the more accurately we measure the velocity of the electron, the less certain we are of the location of the electron, and vice-versa.[92] These quantum mechanics pioneers changed our knowledge of the structure of the atom from Neils Bohr's electron orbits[93] to Schrodinger's electron clouds.

Statistics has a kind of "uncertainty principle" analogous to Heisenberg's—the smaller the amount of data, the less certain we can be of where any single case will show up in the data; the larger the amount of data, the more probable is the prediction of where a particular case will show up in the data. But there is always some possibility that any single case will be an exception to the rule—that it will accidentally fall at the extremities of the "bell-curve".[94] The "bell-curve" is a picture of how a large amount of data will fall around the most common value. There is always an uncertainty about the position of any single datum, even though we have relative certainty of the position where the vast majority of the data will fall.

The discovery of the laws of statistics and probability changed forever the scope of scientific measurement. They are powerful tools that enable scientists to accurately measure the parameters of something that is otherwise unmeasurable—like the position and velocity of an electron. The same statistical tools enable the "soft" sciences of psychology and sociology to measure the unmeasurable—human behavior, for example. The tools of the field of statistics have the uncanny ability to find some kind of order in what looks like random, chaotic behavior. The odd thing about statistics is that there are always exceptions to the rule—occurrences of events not predicted by probability calculations. Much of the data is located outside the middle portion of the "bell curve".[95] One can always find some cases that do not fit the statistical prediction. For the amateur, such exceptions "prove" to them that you can make statistics say whatever you want—statistics are meaningless. But for the experts in the mathematics of statistics, laws of probability can predict how many exceptions there will be and where 95% (or more) of the data will fall—if there is a pattern in the data. Of course, experts will admit that there are many collections of data that have no pattern—nothing but accidental events. But if there is a pattern to be found, the powerful tool of statistical analysis can find it.

Using the wonderful tool of statistics, I was able to publish two studies. One measured the effect of pastoral counseling[96] (using protocols like the one used by Joe Martinus in chapter one and Appendix B, p. 221) on the recidivism rates of delinquent youths following residential treatment. (Recidivism is a measure of how many graduates from a treatment center commit a crime and need to return to a treatment center.) The other study measured the effect of religious activities[97] (like Bible studies) on the recidivism rates. A multiple regression analysis credited 8% of the positive outcome to the religious activities in the latter study[98]. These studies offer scientific evidence for the value of integrating religious activities and pastoral counseling in the residential treatment of delinquent youth. In the last 20 years there has been an explosion of these kinds of sociological studies that offer virtually unanimous evidence for the positive effects of religion on both physical and mental health. Sixteen-hundred of these studies have been collected in the *Handbook of Religion and Health* by Koenig, Larson and McCullough.[99] The vast majority of these studies demonstrate how the tool of statistics can show that in general, religious people live longer lives than non-religious people[100]—even though there are many exceptions to the rule. The power of statistics is the discovery of patterns in data that seem otherwise random. God can have an Intelligent Design in the universe which can include random accidents. It seems that there are accidental events even in God's universe,[101] and yet God is still in control in spite of the accidental events. As we shall see, some of the worst apparent evils in the world are accidents—car accidents, genetic mutations and cataclysmic events (hurricanes, earthquakes, volcanoes, tsunamis, floods, tornadoes, monsoons, fires, etc.)—accidental events that kill and maim innocent people. And there seems to be no "reason" for them. God permits accidents to happen in the universe. Evolution requires genetic accidents (mutations) to happen in order to progress from one species or phylum to another. Accidents are sometimes "good". Understanding bad events as accidental can sometimes offer relief to Jobe Syndrome sufferers. Bad things can happen (accidentally) to good and bad people alike (Matthew 5:45). Bad happenings are not necessarily punishments from God (John 9:2-3).

Chapter Three

Miracles

Miracles are a scandal to many scientists. I have offered a definition of modern science as the quest to explain everything as if God does not exist. That means explaining everything without including miracles. Miracles are usually defined as events that defy the laws of nature. Scientists spend their careers seeking to explain everything by the laws of nature—looking for the Grand Theory of Everything.[102] Violations of the laws of science are not acceptable. But there are other definitions of "miracle". A miracle can be defined as a very improbable event (based on our current knowledge of science). This reminds us of our discussion of statistics and the statistical uncertainty principle—the tool of statistics helps us determine how probable or improbable is an event. We know that very improbable events occur, but they are rare. So too are miracles rare. Statistics discover a pattern in what looks like random events—statistics do not explain the data that do not fit the pattern—they are counted as random accidents requiring no explanation. But miracles are not only improbable events—there is a pattern to their happening. They are the consequences of faith and /or prayer, for example.[103] There are multiple witnesses to faith healing in the

Bible. Jesus often connected his miracles to the faith of the believer: "When Jesus saw their faith" (Matt. 9:2); "Your faith has saved you" (Matt. 9:22); "Let it be done to you according to your faith" (Matt. 9:29); "O woman, great is your faith" (Matt. 15:28). And "he was not able to perform any mighty deed there [Nazareth]... He was amazed at their lack of faith" (Mark. 6:5-6). Some scientists try to explain away the faith factor[104] by describing it as a "placebo effect"—in medical research, the expectation that a treatment will work makes some patients better (even if the treatment was a fake). Likewise, there have been studies done on the effects of prayer for healing.[105] The results have been inconclusive.[106] And the faithful know that there are at least eleven reasons why people are not healed.[107] But the faithful continue to pray for healing even though healings are rare and most of the time, prayer does not bring about major healings. Yet healings do occur—every Catholic saint had to have at least two miracles attributed to their prayer—healings that could not be explained by medical doctors evaluating the cases. "Canonization" of the saints by Pope (saint) John Paul II alone accounts for hundreds of recent, medically evaluated miracles.[108]

There is another definition of miracle. Many miracles are often rather ordinary events that point to an Intelligent Designer—God. For example, the event of human conception happens thousands of times a day. Yet each conception is a miracle that points to infinite Intelligent Design. The more we learn about conception, the more awestruck we become. The human egg cell was discovered only 90 years ago.[109] Prior to that discovery, the common sense belief was that the man planted his seed in the woman. Much simpler. Now we have the benefit of high technology which enables us to view magnified, full color video of the event of conception in the fallopian tube.[110] Now we know about DNA and how the meiosis process produces sex cells with half of the DNA coming from mom and half from dad. Now we know that the combined DNA in the fertilized egg directs the mitosis process to multiply cells and to grow into a human person. Francis Collins, the man who led the team of scientists who mapped the three billion letters in the human genome in 2003[111] converted from atheism to Christianity and called DNA the "*Language of God*".[112] Human conception is a miracle.

Parable of the Lifeboat

Too often do we miss the multitude of everyday miracles while we are looking for the spectacular (and rare) miracles. This is best illustrated in the parable of the lifeboat. This is the story of the man who presumed that God would work a miracle for him during a great flood. "God will come and save me", he said to the neighbors who offered a seat in their car, to the lifeboat that drove up to his house, and to the helicopter pilot who lowered the rope to the man who was now on the roof, waiting for a miracle from God. The man drowned in the flood and when he got to heaven, he complained to God, "Why didn't You save me?" God replied: "I sent you a warning, a car, a lifeboat and a helicopter. What more were you looking for?"[113]

Miracles of Coincidences

Other fairly normal (and often scientific explainable) events can point to Intelligent Design because of their timing. Unbelievers often describe such events as "coincidences"— believers call them "miracles". For example, the History

Channel periodically does a series on the ten plagues of Egypt (based on the Biblical book of Exodus). They offer many possible scientific explanations of how the ten plagues could have naturally occurred. The Bible itself gives some clues to these possibilities. It's not like there never before was a plague of locusts, or frogs, or flies. It was not the first time in history (nor the last) that there was a "black death"[114] nor an epidemic of disease nor a hailstorm nor an eclipse of the sun. The key to the description of these events as "miracles" is primarily the timing of their occurrence—God told Moses to prophesy that these events would happen soon—and they did. And just when the Israelites were backed up to the Red Sea and the army of Pharaoh was in pursuit, there was "a strong easterly wind all night long and he made dry land of the sea" (Exodus 14:22). The tide went out in the nick of time for Israel's crossing and came back in just in time to flood the Egyptians whose chariots were caught in the mud. The tide flow was not unusual—but the timing of it was a miracle. (Without miracles like these, how else can we explain how a slave revolt could have been successful against the most powerful army in the world?)

The Deists

Many of the founding fathers of the United States of America were Deists, including George Washington, Thomas Jefferson, Benjamin Franklin, and James Madison.[115] Deists believe in a creator God who made the universe and its natural laws so perfectly that it continues in existence and harmony forever without the need of any intervention—no need for a Messiah, prophet or revelation of any kind. Thus, Deists are Theists—believers in God. But they are not considered

Christians—believers in Jesus the Christ. And the Deists do not believe in miracles—only natural laws. And God does not violate the natural laws he created. So the Deist's God is one that many scientists believe in—because God set up the natural laws and does not violate or suspend them—and the natural laws are the objects of scientific discovery and investigation. Perhaps 90% of the time, Christians experience the universe like the Deists—everything seems to proceed according to predictable natural laws. But Christians hold on to the memory of the great miracles of the Bible and especially to the great intervention of God at the beginning of the first millennium A.D., when the Son of God became man—and they hold on to the faith that their prayers make a difference in their world.

Five Gaps in Scientific Knowledge

As we have seen above, even though an event happens thousands of times a day, it can be called a miracle when its complexity points to a Creator. And even though an event has a natural scientific explanation, it can be called a miracle when the timing of the event points to Divine Providence. And God could have behaved like the Deists claim—God could have created the world according to natural laws that are never broken—if God wanted to. Yet even if God did refuse to intervene in history, there are still at least five events unexplained by science—five gaps in our scientific knowledge requiring the intervention of an Intelligent Designer—a "God-of-the Gaps".

1) The animation of the first living cell from organic chemicals.

2) The consciousness of the first human surpassing all primates.
3) The Anthropic universe
4) DNA
5) The existence of altruism—unselfishness—in any human community.

In fact, each of these events seems to violate natural laws. The 1st two seem to violate the second law of thermodynamics—entropy (disorder) inevitably increases. A living cell is a significant increase in order and complexity of chemicals; human consciousness has created a miraculously complex and ordered world out of the wilderness of planet earth. Both of these events at least temporarily violate the direction of entropy—the force toward chaos. (Remember that some scientists dismiss the thermodynamics by stating that these laws do not apply to an "open system"—one without boundaries blocking energy exchanges. They claim that the universe is an open system.[116] But the evidence supports the opposite claim—the universe is a "closed system"—it has a boundary, though an expanding one.[117]) The third event—the Anthropic Universe—a universe perfectly "designed" or "programmed" to produce and sustain human Life—exists in spite of astronomical odds against its existence. The 4th event—the existence of DNA—is the discovery of the language of a Supreme Intelligent Being (God), hidden but now discovered in every living cell. All of these events continue to transcend scientific explanation.

The fifth event—the existence of altruism—also seems to violate the theory of evolution. Evolution theory is based on two assumptions: random genetic mutations and natural selection. Natural selection chooses the most "fit" muta-tions for survival—"survival of the fittest". There is no room for altruism in evolution. Selfishness is supposed to explain all evolutionary events. Even the DNA in every cell is selfish. Atheist scientist Richard Dawkins[118] wrote the book on *The Selfish Gene.*[119] Therefore, the existence of altruism—unself-ishness—seems to violate evolution theory. Socio-biologists try to explain human altruism by studying the ant and bee col-onies. These colonies have many members who sacrifice their own lives for the good of the community. However, Socio-biologists' attempts fail to explain any altruism in insects that do not have genes in common. All the bees in the hive share the genes of the Queen. So the worker bees instinctively sacrifice their lives for the colony. The selfish gene explains the apparent altruism of the beehive. Not so for humans. Altruism of mothers and fathers for their children or siblings or parents can be explained by genetics—the common genes of family members produce an altruism based on instinct, not on choice. But the altruism of Jesus (and his disciples), for example—sacrifice of one's life for non-relatives—Is a vio-lation of evolution theory. (Luke 6:31-35; Matthew 12:48-50).

In his controversial keynote address as president of the American Psychological Association (August, 1975), Donald T. Campbell, professor of psychology at Northwestern University, challenged his peers to engage in a respectful dialogue with religious leaders with an aim to eliminate the

> ...conflict between psychology and tradition... psychologists almost invariably side with self-gratification over traditional restraint... psychology may be contributing to the

undermining of the retention of what may be extremely valuable... which we do not yet fully understand... I would recommend that as an initial approach we assume an underlying wisdom in the recipes for living with which tradition has supplied us... frequently, psychology does reduce obedience to traditional moral standards, no doubt often in ways genuinely therapeutic but more often in ways dysfunctional... [120]

When Campbell speaks of the "tradition", he is referring to religion and religious cultures that are examples of social evolution where the "recipes for living" (morals and ethics) replace the genes of biological evolution. Human selection of superior recipes for living over the centuries has produced wisdom that has been tried and tested (as opposed to the selfish ethics of psychology which form the basis of untested social experiments). The recipes for living contained in the traditions motivate a high degree of altruism that cannot be explained by genetics.

I see humankind as the only vertebrate that approaches the social insects in self-sacrificial altruism... because for humans there is genetic competition among the cooperators, this extreme sociality cannot have been achieved on a genetic basis......social evolution has had to counter individual selfish tendencies which biological evolution has continued to select...[121]

Altruism (unselfishness) is a virtue so necessary to the survival of cultures around the world and it cannot come from the selfish genes of biological evolution. The existence of altruism cannot be explained by genetics. It remains as a significant gap in materialistic, atheistic world views.

All five gaps in scientific knowledge point to an Intelligent and Benevolent Designer, a metaphysical reality we call God. Each of these gaps will be treated in greater detail in subsequent chapters. Theories will be described that will help to fill in these gaps in current scientific thought. Much of what I present will be digested material from other authors. Some will be new ideas. But all of this material will be shown to be helpful to both the religious person as well as the scientist, and to anyone struggling with Jobe Syndrome.

Scientists do not like miracles because they are unpredictable. Scientific theories earn their prestige and credibility by how successful they are in predicting events. Scientific theories should be able to predict events. The theories I include in this book will be shown to have predicted many events and in so doing qualify them to be considered as consistent with the scientific method. This method will focus especially on the definition of miracles as events which point to meaning, purpose and communication in the wonderful awesome complexity and order that has been programmed in our universe by an Intelligent and Benevolent Designer-God.

Brother Sun, Sister Moon

(Note to the reader: Chapter four attempts to translate some of the language of physics and chemistry into common language. If you get bogged down in this language, please proceed to chapter 5, Mother Earth (page 76).)

St. Francis of Assisi was a nature-lover. He was awestruck with wonder at creation. His love for creation (and for the Creator) is expressed in the poem-prayer he wrote:

Most high, all powerful, all good Lord!
All praise is Yours, all glory, all honor, and
all blessing.
To You, alone, Most High, do they belong.
No mortal lips are worthy to pronounce
Your name.
Be praised, my Lord, through all Your creatures,
especially through my lord **Brother Sun**,
who brings the day; and You give light
through him.
And he is beautiful and radiant in all his splendor!

Of You, Most High, he bears the likeness.
Be praised, my Lord, through **Sister Moon** and
the stars;
in the heavens You have made them bright, precious and beautiful.
Be praised, my Lord, through **Brothers
Wind and Air**,
and clouds and storms, and all the weather,
through which You give Your creatures
sustenance.
Be praised, my Lord, through **Sister Water**;
she is very useful, and humble, and precious,
and pure.
Be praised, my Lord, through **Brother Fire**,
through whom You brighten the night.
He is beautiful and cheerful, and powerful
and strong.
Be praised, my Lord, through **our sister
Mother Earth**,
who feeds us and rules us,
and produces various fruits with colored flowers
and herbs.
Be praised, my Lord, through those who forgive
for love of You;
through those who endure **sickness and trial**.
Happy those who endure in peace,
for by You, Most High, they will be crowned.
Be praised, my Lord, through **our sister
Bodily Death**,
from whose embrace no living person
can escape.
Woe to those who die in **mortal sin**!

Happy those she finds doing Your most holy will.
The **second death** can do no harm to them.
Praise and bless my Lord, and give thanks,
and serve Him with great humility.[122]

This book attempts to reveal the wonder and awe of St. Francis at the universe and its Designer. In so doing, it will use St. Francis' prayer as an outline, endeavoring—as he did—to find meaning and purpose and design and communication in the universe and its Designer. I have added a chapter on Brother Pain to address "those who endure sickness and trial". Those of you struggling with Jobe Syndrome will hopefully find the chapters on Brother Pain and Sister Death especially helpful. You may need to jump to those chapters now. Meanwhile, this chapter will begin at the beginning—the Big Bang that produced Brother Sun and Sister Moon.

When discussions point to a Designer of the universe to explain where it came from, some skeptics challenge the Theist with the question: "But where did God come from?"[123] My discussion avoids the speculation on what existed at the beginning of the universe—eternal matter and energy? Black hole? Metaphysical God? Our discussion invites the skeptic to describe the substance of what existed "in the beginning". You name it. No matter what you describe as what always was, I will respond—OK, you say (for example) that matter and energy always existed without beginning and without end. I say, OK. But I am compelled by the evidence to add that this Matter and Energy is animated by an Intelligence. Or if the universe began as a Black Hole, I am compelled by the evidence to say, the Black Hole that was the origin of the universe is animated by an Intelligence. And I am also compelled by the evidence to add that the origin of the universe is Benevolent (caring and kind). What is the evidence?

If the universe is animated by Intelligence, I would be able to predict that I could find evidence of intelligence in it. What would evidence of intelligence look like? It would look like the same kind of evidence used in the science of archeology— cave drawings, hieroglyphics, tools, crafts, language, etc. In fact, we could theorize that some similar discovery of evidence occurred between the first cave men, cave "persons". How did the first cave person discover that there was another cave person? He looked into her eyes and experienced her spirit / soul. He watched her behavior and found signs of intelligence far above the animals. He saw her drawings, her tools, her crafts, her sign language. He knew that she was far more intelligent than the other animals. And the more complex the drawing, the tool, the craft, the language, the more intelligent the object. Indeed, the other object was not only an object, she was a person, a very intelligent person with a consciousness like his—far above the animals. So too, the archeologist digs for the same kind of evidence. How can the archeologist discern which discoveries are evidence for intelligence and which are not? She looks for purpose and meaning in the artifacts—a definite ordering of the environment that is extremely improbable to have occurred by accident, by random events. Randomness, chaos, highly probable disorder of particles, earth, rocks, etc.—all of these are signs of non-intelligence. Common sense (and the second law of thermodynamics) tells us that over time, everything naturally disintegrates, wears down, falls apart, breaks into pieces (entropy inevitably increases), unless an intelligent being intervenes and puts things in order, repairs the breakage, re-builds the object, etc. Meaning and purpose are keys to intelligence and language is always evidence of it. The more complex the design, the purpose, the language, the more intelligent must be the Designer.

Take for example the moon landing. Astronauts set foot on Sister Moon for the first time in 1969. The environment on the moon was just as expected—no marks of intelligent life at all. All the marks on the lunar surface appeared to have no meaning or purpose, no order or complexity. If there had been order, the force of entropy eliminated it over time. All of the indentations in the moon dust appear to be the result of random crashes of meteors large and small—the key word being "random". The astronauts collected their samples of inanimate moon dust and returned home. The historic moon landing was a phenomenal success of human technology.

But what if the astronauts would have found arrowheads, clay pots, hatchet-heads, feathered headdresses, geometric and symmetric decorations on some clay pots and drawings of stick men or animals on others? What would be the headline? Of course, it would be, "Astronauts discover artifacts of an ancient civilization on the surface of the moon!!!" This would have been not only a common-sense conclusion of moon visitors—this would have been a scientific conclusion of archeologists and paleontologists. Articles would have appeared in scientific peer-reviewed journals. We finally discovered evidence of aliens.

But what if NASA had kept our moon landing a secret? And what if the Russians had landed on the moon after the Americans did? The Russians would have found the "moon-rover"[124] and what would they have concluded? "The complex vehicle is a product of millions of years of random collisions of particles and natural selection of movable parts that enable the object to move under its own power?" Absolutely not! No one in their right mind would come to such a conclusion. Common sense folks would be like the archeologists and paleontologists who would say, "Intelligent life has been on the moon before us!" Perhaps the news headlines would say, "Evidence of aliens on the moon!"

In spite of all this kind of common-sense knowledge and scientific methodology, doesn't the atheistic scientist claim, "Humans are nothing but the product of random collisions of particles and natural selection of objects that are the fittest to survive. There is no design and no Designer?" The second law of thermodynamics does not apply because of the atheist scientist's (metaphysical and faith-based) claim that the universe is an "open system". The atheist scientist is operating in the realm of metaphysics, not physics and basing his conclusions on faith rather than evidence. The evidence so far shows that the universe is expanding but it has a boundary—all energy and matter that we know of had been contained in the black hole at the moment of the Big Bang. And it continues to be bound by gravity in the expanding but limited universe. The universe is a closed system and the laws of thermodynamics apply to it, including the law of increasing entropy—increasing chaos and disorder—and the evolution process has been violating the "thermodynamic arrow"[125], begging for an explanation. How could something like a moon rover or a laptop computer assemble itself on the moon? Natural selection and random mutation? Impossible. Or, in more scientific language, extremely improbable. But the probabilities shift dramatically if an intelligent being has been on the moon. The laptop is a possible tool of an intelligent alien or a human or some being at least as intelligent as a human.

But what about the solar system? What about the universe? Are these the nothing but the random accidents of the Big Bang? Or is there evidence for a Super Intelligence? Is the universe the product of an Intelligent Designer? The preponderance of the evidence will point to "yes". And the most visible, most significant piece of evidence for Intelligent Design is looking at me in the mirror—the heads of human beings are the most complex and advanced "computers" in the world—we are the most sophisticated "robots" ever assembled. How could such beings ever become "assembled"? Only by something—Someone—much more intelligent than humans—a super-intelligent Designer. It's just like the sciences of archeology and paleontology—when you uncover the "tools" of the beings, the objects that have meaning and purpose, the evidence of language or artworks, you conclude that intelligent life was there. If you discover a laptop in a time-capsule, you know that a high-tech culture had left it behind. If you discover a human being on planet earth, you know that a super-intelligent Designer exists. But let's begin at the beginning—what are all the signs of intelligence in the universe? They are best summed up in the phrase, "anthropic principle".

The Anthropic Principle

The anthropic principle is a huge challenge for the atheist-scientist. It was a huge challenge for Stephen Hawking, for example. It is a significant part of both of his books.[126] The best definition of the anthropic principle is this—the evidence seems to show that the universe is carefully and purposely designed to create and sustain human life. (*Anthropos* is the Greek word for "man".) Hawking defines the "Anthropic Principle" as follows:

> "We see the universe the way it is because we exist."

> There are two versions of the anthropic principle, the weak and the strong. The weak anthropic principle states that in a universe that is large or infinite in space and / or time, the conditions necessary for the development of intellectual life will be met only in certain regions that are limited in space and time...

> Some, however, go much further and propose a strong version of the principle... the laws of science, as we know them at present, contain many fundamental numbers... The remarkable fact is that the values of these numbers seem to have been very finely adjusted to make possible the development of life... Most sets of values would give rise to universes that, although they might be very beautiful, would contain no one able to wonder at that beauty. One can take this either as evidence of a divine purpose in Creation and the choice of the laws of science or as support for the strong anthropic principle.[127]

Hawking refuses to accept this strong version of the anthropic principle. "…it runs against the tide of the whole history of science". Yes, it does, because the whole history of science can be considered as an attempt to explain everything without appealing to a Creator God…

> …the strong anthropic principle would claim that this whole vast construction exists simply for our sake. This is very hard to believe.[128]

Yes, it is unbelievable. It means that every human being has won the lottery—several times!

> This means that the initial state of the universe must have been carefully chosen indeed if the hot big bang model was correct right back to the beginning of time. It would be very difficult to explain why the universe should have begun in just this way, except as the act of a God who intended to create beings like us.[129]

Such comments by Hawking in his 1988 book might suggest that he is a Deist—a believer in a creator God who set up the universe perfectly and then let it run on its own forever after.

> Science seems to have uncovered a set of laws that… may have originally been decreed by God, but it appears that he has since left the universe to evolve according to them and does not now intervene in it… the whole history of science has been the gradual realization that events do not happen in an arbitrary manner,

but that they reflect a certain underlying order, which may or may not be divinely inspired.[130]

This paragraph shows a half-hearted respect for Deism—but Hawking's career not only reduces God to a Deist Creator who is no longer needed after he set up the universe; Hawking's goal is to discover the grand theory of everything that would eliminate even the need for any creator at all.

> The idea that space and time may form a closed surface without boundary also has profound implications for the role of God in the affairs of the universe. With the success of the scientific theories in describing events, most people have come to believe that God allows the universe to evolve according to a set of laws and does not intervene in the universe to break these laws… it would still be up to God to wind up the clockwork and choose how to start it off. So long as the universe had a beginning we could suppose it had a creator. But if the universe is really completely self-contained, having no boundary or edge, it would have neither beginning nor end: it would simply be. What place, then, for a creator?[131]

In his 1988 book, Hawking predicted that the grand theory would be discovered that would eliminate the need for a creator. But even if the grand theory explained what the universe would look like without a creator, Hawking admitted that it would not answer the question, "Why?"

The usual approach of science of constructing a mathematical model cannot answer the questions of why there should be a universe for the model to describe. Why does the universe go to all the bother of existing? Is the unified theory so compelling that it brings about its own existence? Or does it need a creator, and, if so, does he have any other effect on the universe? And who created him?[132]

However, if we do discover a complete theory, it should in time be understandable in broad principle by everyone, not just a few scientists. Then we shall all, philosophers, scientists, and just ordinary people, be able to take part in the discussion of the question of why it is that we and the universe exist. If we find the answer to that, it would be the ultimate triumph of human reason—for then we would know the mind of God.[133]

Hawking shows more humility in this book than he does in his 2010 book, *The Grand Design*. In this latter book, he does admit that the quest for the grand theory of everything has not yet been successful. In fact, science should perhaps accept the possibility that there is no such theory.

But no single theory within the network can describe every aspect of the universe—all the forces of nature, the particles that feel those forces, and the frame work of space and time in which it all plays out. Though this situation

> does not fulfill the traditional physicists' dream
> of a single unified theory, it is acceptable within
> the framework of model-dependent realism.[134]

The best possible candidate for the grand theory is the M-theory, but Hawking is not optimistic about its ability to unify all theories.

> That more fundamental theory is called
> M-theory... no one seems to know what the "M"
> stands for, but it may be "master", "miracle", or
> "mystery". It seems to be all three. People are
> still trying to decipher the nature of M-theory,
> but that may not be possible. It could be that
> the physicists' traditional expectation of a
> single theory of nature is untenable, and there
> exists no single formulation.[135]

This seems to be a humble admission that the grand theory of everything has thus far been elusive and may not be possible at all. [136] And Hawking continued to acknowledge the "anthropic principle"—the universe seems to have been carefully designed to produce human life—until his death on March 14, 2018.

> The weak anthropic principle is not very con-
> troversial. But there is a stronger form that
> we will argue for here, although it is regarded
> with disdain among some physicists. The
> strong anthropic principle suggests that the
> fact that we exist imposes restraints not just
> on our *environment* but on the possible *form*

and content of the laws of nature themselves. The idea arose because it is not only the peculiar characteristics of our solar system that seem oddly conducive to the development of human life but also the characteristics of our entire universe, and that is much more difficult to explain.[137]

Hawking goes on to enumerate the many forces and constants in the universe that, if altered only minutely, would make life impossible. It seems like Hawking is on the threshold of theism.

Our universe and its laws appear to have a design that both is tailor-made to support us, and, if we are to exist, leaves little room for alteration. That is not easily explained, and raises the natural question of why it is that way.

Many people would like us to use these coincidences as evidence of the work of God.[138]

But Hawking refuses to go there. In spite of the "overwhelming evidence for purpose and design found in modern science"[139], Hawking maintains his metaphysical faith in science as providing an explanation of everything without appealing to God.

But the discovery relatively recently of the extreme fine tuning of so many of the laws of nature could lead at least some of us back to the old idea that this grand design is the work of some grand designer… with the unstated but implied understanding that the designer is God.

That is not the answer of modern science.[140]

How does Hawking deny the "overwhelming evidence for purpose and design" (and the Designer)? He takes refuge in the metaphysical belief that there are "multiverses", billions of universes, each of which has millions of planets like earth and thousands of cultures of intelligent life (aliens)[141]. It's kind of like the belief that if I play the lottery every day for 10 million years, I will probably win the lottery someday. Hawking's belief is that the theory of multiverses somehow explains how we won the cosmological lottery—how we by pure luck emerged on planet earth. He considers this theory as momentous and as historic as the theory of evolution.

But just as Darwin and Wallace explained how the apparently miraculous design of living forms could appear without intervention by a supreme being, the multiverse concept can explain the fine-tuning of physical law without the need for a benevolent creator who made the universe for our benefit.[142]

It is interesting that Hawking places the M-theory alongside evolution as a triumph in the assault on theism by atheism (explaining everything without God). As we have alluded to above and as we will elaborate in detail below (in the chapter on Mother Earth), in spite of nearly 150 years of research and successes in the explanation of multi-forms of life, that same gap in the evolution theory—failing to explain the transition of organic chemicals to a living cell—remains. And the discovery of DNA is equivalent to the discovery of a manufacturer's instructions for the construction of a living cell. Some historians of science call DNA the "Language of God".[143] Hawking is right to juxtapose the two momentous events. Both illustrate the same anthropic principle—it seems like the universe has been programmed to produce human life. How can there be a program without a programmer? How can we explain the design without a designer?

> Some would claim the answer to these questions is that there is a God who chose to create the universe that way. It is reasonable to ask who or what created the universe, but if the answer is God, then the question has merely been deflected to that of who created God. In this view it is accepted that some entity exists that needs no creator, and that entity is called God. This is known as the first-cause argument for the existence of God. We claim, however, that it is possible to answer these questions purely within the realm of science, and without invoking any divine beings.[144]

Hawking believes in aliens[145] but he refuses to believe in God. It is like us landing on Mars and finding a computer and concluding that there must be alien intelligence there—and then, finding an intelligent alien, concluding that the alien origin happened by chance collision of particles over millions of years. Which is more believable? That the computer was assembled by random collisions of particles over millions of years or that the alien was assembled by random collisions of particles over millions of years? Or is it more believable to conclude that both the computer and the alien were created by (an) intelligent designer(s)? Common sense suggests that the latter conclusion is more believable. And many scientists and philosophers of science agree.

The anthropic principle has converted some scientists from atheism to theism (at least in its Deist form). Hawking mentions at least one of them in his book—Fred Hoyle. He is mentioned alongside Father George Lemaitre, Roman Catholic priest and physics professor, as co-inventors of the Big Bang theory.[146] Hoyle was an atheist-astrophysicist, and even though the Big Bang theory is significant evidence for a creation event (and a creator), that did not deter him from atheism. What did convert him was the anthropic principle—Fred Hoyle discovered how precise the parameters had to be for a star to produce any atoms larger than helium—atoms like carbon and oxygen and nitrogen—so important to living cells.

> ...a change of as little as 0.5 percent in the strength of the strong nuclear force, or 4 percent in the electric force, would destroy either nearly all carbon or all oxygen in every star, and hence the possibility of life as we know it... if the other nuclear force, the weak force, were much weaker, in the early universe all the hydrogen in the cosmos would have turned to helium, and hence there would be no normal stars... if protons were 0.2 percent heavier, they would decay into neutrons, destabilizing atoms.[147]

Hoyle wrote: "I do not believe that any scientist who examined the evidence would fail to draw the inference that the laws of nuclear physics have been deliberately designed with regard to the consequences they produce inside the stars."[148]

Hawking does not mention Hoyle's use of the term "super-intellect" to explain the anthropic principle nor the title of Hoyle's book, *The Intelligent Universe*.[149] This sounds too much like a theist scientist's language. But below are Hoyle's own words (as quoted in Spitzer).[150]

… A common sense interpretation of the facts suggests that a super-intellect has monkeyed with physics, as well as with chemistry and biology, and that there are no blind forces worth speaking about in nature. The numbers one calculates from the facts seem to me so overwhelming as to put this conclusion almost beyond question.[151]

Stephen Meyer claimed that Fred Hoyle is also famous for comparing "the problem of getting life to arise spontaneously from its constituent parts to the problem of getting a 747 airplane to come together from a tornado swirling through a junk yard."[152]

The Intelligent Design explanation of the anthropic principle has persuaded many other scientists beside Hoyle. Philosopher of Science, Father Robert Spitzer, names at least

seven scientists who demonstrate "remarkable openness...
to the prospect of supernatural design":

> Contemporary physicists such as Arno
> Penzias, Roger Penrose, Owen Gingerich,
> John Polkinghorne, Fred Hoyle, and Paul
> Davies have since adduced the plausibility of
> a designing intelligence from the evidence of
> contemporary physics.[153]

Roger Penrose teamed up with Stephen Hawking to prove that
the Big Bang occurred.[154] Robert Spitzer quotes Paul Davies:

> ...the numerical coincidences [necessary for
> an anthropic universe] could be regarded as
> evidence of design. The delicate fine-tuning in
> the values of the constants, necessary so that
> the various different branches of physics can
> dovetail so felicitously, might be attributed to
> God... the seemingly miraculous concurrence
> of numerical values that nature has assigned
> to her fundamental constants must remain as
> the most compelling evidence for an element
> of cosmic design.[155]

This is one kind of miracle that I mentioned in chapter 3—not
violating natural laws, but the existence of the laws themselves point to a lawgiver. Robert Spitzer quotes "Nobel
prize-winning physicist" Arno Penzias:

> Astronomy leads us to a unique event, a uni-
> verse which was created out of nothing, and

deliberately balanced to provide exactly the conditions required to support life. In the absence of an absurdly improbable accident, the observations of modern science seem to suggest an underlying, one might say, super-natural plan.[156]

Spitzer notes that Polkinghorne quoted Freeman Dyson's words:

"The more I examine the universe and the details of its architecture, the more evidence that I find that the universe in some sense must have known we were coming." [Polkinghorne comments:] I cannot see what sense that could be other than the will of a Creator.[157]

What are the elements that we are referring to when we speak of an "anthropic universe"—a universe that seems to have been designed with a purpose to produce human life? They are the total opposite of what we could expect. What we could expect in an un-designed universe is chaos and totally random collisions of particles with no direction or purpose. Robert Spitzer quotes Albert Einstein:

You find it strange that I consider the compre-hensibility of the world to the degree that we may speak of such comprehensibility as a mir-acle or an eternal mystery. Well, *a priori* one should expect a chaotic world which cannot be in any way grasped through thought... the kind of order created, for example, by Newton's

> theory of gravity…presupposes an order in the objective world of a high degree which one has no *a priori* right to expect. That is the "miracle" which grows increasingly persuasive with the increasing development of knowledge.[158]

Einstein claims that the "order" in the objective world is a "mystery" and a "miracle". "*A priori*" means prior to investigation—what we can know about something before we begin to investigate it. We know *a priori* that we could not ever be successful with the scientific method if the universe did not have any objective order or follow any laws—all the objects in our world could behave in a totally random fashion, like they do in our dreams. But we have been amazingly successful with the scientific method precisely because the universe does follow laws that do not change—the behavior of objects in our universe is consistent with order and purpose—in spite of the apparent randomness of particle collisions and the "uncertainty principles". In some sense, it is a good thing that miracles are rare events.

"Relativism" does not work

The contemporary secular world tends to believe in "Relativism" more than scientific objectivism, rejecting the "order in the objective world" that Einstein mentioned above. Or more accurately, relativism is more popular with regard to lifestyle while scientific objectivity is presumed to be correct in the fields of science. However, the two world views cannot both be true. Relativism claims that truth is not objective—truth is relative to every person's perspective. Each person has his or her own truth, and no one has the right to question his or her truth. There is no such thing as objective truth (except in science?). Former-atheist philosopher Anthony Flew calls the relativist a "solipsist" who rejects the existence of any truth but his own.[159] But the relativist's truth is contradictory—"there is no objective truth"—in other words, the relativist's "truth" is not true. In effect, the relativist is saying, "The 'truth' I am stating is not true. In other words, he is saying, "There is only one objective truth and it is this—there is no objective truth (except for the one "truth" that I just stated). The relativist cuts off the very limb on which he is standing. Relativism does not work. It must be rejected in favor of Einstein's "order in the objective world". It is a "mystery" and a "miracle" that we can discover the order built into the universe. We can know objective truth and the human task is to uncover it. And among the fruits of this human endeavor are the laws of science.

The Anthropic Universe

The laws of the universe involve many key numbers that are called "constants". They are called constants because they are not variables—they do not change values in the equations that define the laws of the universe. If they were variable, the universe would collapse. In fact, if these numbers were only very slightly altered, the universe as we know it would not be possible. Robert Spitzer counted 20 of these constants:

- 4 constants related to space and time (including the speed of light);
- 8 constants related to the forces of nature (including the gravity constant);

- 8 other constants that "refine… interactions among the above 12".[160]

Out of the 20 constants, Spitzer highlights "seven instances of this narrow range of constant values necessary for our anthropic universe"[161]:

- Our universe happens to have very low entropy / high complexity and order. Roger Penrose (partner with Stephen Hawking on the proof of the Big Bang event[162]) calculated the odds of our anthropic universe with very low entropy / chaos (and very high order) arising out of all the possible universes to be one chance out of an astronomic number of possibilities— the number one with 120 zeros after it![163] Penrose's number doesn't fit on one line of this page (each line has about 84 letters, digits and spaces).

- Paul Davies calculated that if the gravitational constant and the weak force constant were changed by even one part in an astronomic number—the number one with 50 zeros behind it—"the structure of the universe would be drastically altered";[164]

- "Brandon Carter in 1970 showed that a 2% reduction in the strong force and its associated constant would preclude the formation of nuclei with larger numbers of protons…making the formation of elements heavier than hydrogen impossible…leaving the universe no water"[165];

- Paul Davies described "an extraordinary coincidence" of the precise balance of neutron, proton and electron masses—very slight differences in these numbers would have eliminated hydrogen atoms or atoms larger than helium, situations "inhospitable to life"[166];

- The delicate balance between the gravitational constant, the electromagnetic constant, the electron and proton masses is such that "without these precise values the vast majority of the stars would have been blue giants or red dwarfs (unable to sustain a life form)"[167];

- "A sixth instance of the improbability of anthropic conditions concerns the weak force constant… if the weak force had varied ever so slightly, supernovae would never have occurred, thereby depriving carbon atoms of the heat necessary for their production."[168] And without carbon atoms there is no life possible that we know of.

- The seventh instance of a miraculous coincidence has been mentioned above. Fred Hoyle predicted this coincidence, that the resonance of the atomic nuclei of carbon "happens to coincide perfectly with the resonances of beryllium, helium and oxygen. If this extremely remote coincidence had not occurred, then carbon would be extremely rare, and carbon-based life forms would not have emerged… nothing has shaken [Fred Hoyle's] atheism as much as this discovery"[169]

The existence of Brother Sun and Sister Moon would have been impossible without these and many other amazing coincidences of nature. And, of course, without Brother Sun, Planet Earth would not exist, nor would any life forms, let alone human life as we know it. Every one of us humans on Planet Earth has won the life lottery—many times over. The atheist calls us extremely lucky—theists call us extremely blessed. Our universe is Anthropic—it has been programmed to produce and sustain human life. The Designer of the Universe must be Benevolent as well as Intelligent —God cares about us.

An argument for Anthropy can be outlined as a syllogism as follows:

- All of the physical constants in the universe appear to be finely-tuned to produce and support life

- Fine-tuning is evidence for the existence of a Fine-Tuner / Intelligent Designer

- Therefore, the universe must have been created by a Supreme Intelligent Designer

Robert Spitzer's syllogism for the beginning of the universe follows:

- If there is a reasonable likelihood of a beginning of the universe (prior to which there was no physical reality whatsoever), and

- If it is a priori true that "from nothing, only nothing comes,"

- Then it is reasonably likely that the universe came from *something* which is *not* physical reality. This is commonly referred to as a "transcendent cause of the universe (physical reality)" or "a creator of the universe."[170]

(See Appendix C on page 224 for outlines of all the arguments in the book.)

CHAPTER FIVE

Mother Earth

(Note to the reader: Chapter five attempts to translate some of the language of bio-chemistry and micro-biology into common language. If you get bogged down in this language, please proceed to chapter 6, Predictions (page 102).)

M other Earth is the extremely rare planet the likes of which we have not yet discovered—and we may never discover. As we have seen above, the odds of finding a universe that is programmed to produce a planet like Mother Earth and to produce human life are astronomically low. Yet our Brother Sun and Sister Moon emerged from the Big Bang and Mother Earth was caught in a gravitational field in precisely the right orbit to have a year-round tropical zone whose rain forests became a cradle of life. Mother Earth is a perfect environment to create and nurture life. But it was not so in the beginning. The Big Bang occurred 13.8 billion years ago and it took 10 billion years to produce the first living cell[171]. What was Mother Earth like during those 10 billion years? Scientists believe the planet did not form until about 4 billion years ago and it was extremely hot and uninhabitable.[172] Mother Earth gradually cooled, eventually leading to the Ice Age. In the process of these monumental changes in Planet Earth, tectonic plates ground together, volcanoes spewed molten rock from the earth's core and oceans changed sizes and shapes to form Planet Earth into the beautiful, awesome habitat of mountains, rivers, oceans and prairies, rain forests and rich black earth and slime, fertile and ready for life. The process of change involved what today we call cataclysmic events, often with tragic results for life—earthquakes, volcanoes, tsunamis, tornadoes, hurricanes, monsoons, etc. But these cataclysmic events enabled the natural process of the evolution of Planet Earth into Mother Earth—they enabled life to evolve. These cataclysmic events were good things! But once Planet Earth became Mother Earth and human life eventually evolved, suddenly people considered the cataclysmic events to be "bad"—"evils" to be feared—the "wrath" of God. What once were "good" natural events became "evil". Why?

The Tapestry

The tapestry is a helpful model to use for life. It is a model that finds design in apparent chaos. Rabbi Kushner credited Thornton Wilder with the first use of the model.[173] A tapestry is an elaborate, complex interweaving of colored threads that are designed by a Designer to create a beautiful picture (like the one in Image 6):

Image 6 is a beautiful picture on one side. But if you look at the backside of an authentic tapestry, the picture is unrecognizable—a tangled, chaotic, blurred mess of colored threads with no apparent design or order. See Image 7.

Image 7:

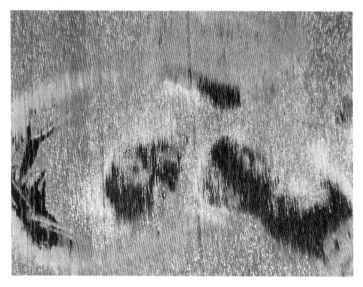

Often the chaotic backside of the tapestry is covered with cloth to hide the chaos. But it is the apparent tangle of threads on the backside enables them to form the beautiful picture on the frontside. The beautiful picture is God's perspective—reality as it is seen by the Designer. But in human experience, the frontside is mostly invisible (until death)—the frontside is hidden. It is the backside that we see. The tapestry is a great model for human experience. Our human perspective on life is limited—we cannot see the big picture, the forest—we see only trees. We see the backside of the tapestry, the chaotic side. Many life events seem to be totally chaotic, not so beautiful, accidents that cause us suffering, pain, disease and death. They seem to be totally evil. How could anything good come from them? We experience Jobe Syndrome. We ask God, "Why?" Some people say, "There is always a reason." I agree with Rabbi Harold Kushner that sometimes there is no reason—there are such things as accidents.[174] But I disagree with the Rabbi about the tapestry—the Rabbi doesn't like this model. But his primary reason to reject the tapestry model is that no one has ever seen it.[175] But models are models, not reality. They are things we can look at that help us to understand reality. They are like parables or metaphors. The tapestry model helps us to understand the reality underlying Jobe Syndrome—events that seem chaotic and accidental can produce something beautiful. Even things that are evil can be used to make something good. The messy backside of life can be seen as beautiful from another perspective. And even if we can't say, "There is always a reason", we can say that God can help us get through bad events and to grow stronger, more beautiful or productive. I think that the proverb, "God can draw straight with crooked lines", is a helpful cliché. Better than, "There is always a reason."

The best insight of Rabbi Kushner is his bottom-line answer to the question, "What good is God?" (if God doesn't answer our prayer or protect us from accidents, pain, suffering and death). His answer is, "God suffers along with us." The Rabbi claims that "Christianity introduced the world to the idea of a God who suffers".[176] Cardinal Robert Sarah states it this way: "To believe in a God who "suffers" is to make the mystery of God's silence more mysterious and more luminous, too."[177] He quotes a letter from a mother who related her own experience of suffering over the bad choices of her children, to God's suffering: "This way I manage to glimpse the fact that God the "Father" can suffer."[178] I believe along with the Cardinal that this message is a most important one for anyone suffering from Jobe Syndrome—God feels your pain. "And Jesus Wept" (John 11:35). I propose the tapestry model to help understand sometimes why there is pain. And this book is intended to offer evidence and clues for the reality of the beautiful picture on the frontside.

The cataclysmic events that formed our planet did not become "bad" or "evil" when Planet Earth became Mother Earth. They are still "good" and necessary for sustaining the planet. They follow the same natural laws that they have always followed since the universe was designed. These natural laws are good and beautiful and true. It's just that once life evolved, the possibility of death came with it—and cataclysmic events can cause death. According to the tapestry model, we see the backside where the image is blurred and chaotic and it seems ugly and evil. There is evil in God's world—evil not made by God. But we can believe that on the frontside of the tapestry there is a beautiful picture. Even death has a beautiful side (but that is coming in chapter nine, Sister Death).

Evolution and Entropy

I have noted above how improbable it was that we would happen to find ourselves in a low entropy, highly ordered universe—we won the lottery. We can now apply the same laws of thermodynamics to Planet Earth to discover how improbable it was that Planet Earth became Mother Earth—how improbable it was that life happened. We noted above how the concept of Entropy in the second law of thermodynamics is a measure of chaos and disorder, and that all natural processes tend to increase entropy—to increase chaos and disorder (in a closed system). In a real sense, entropy, then, is a measure of "fitness" for survival. The objects most "fit" to survive are high entropy (chaotic) objects without order. And in this sense, there is a significant relationship between entropy and Darwin's concept of "Natural Selection". Natural selection is the concept of "survival of the fittest"—living things have come into existence and continue to exist because they are more suited to survive than their ancient counterparts that died out because they were less fit for survival.[179] The complementary concept is "random mutation". "Random mutations arise in the genome of an individual organism, and offspring can inherit such mutations."[180] Gene reproduction is apparently not a perfect process—there are accidental "mistakes" in the copying of genes. Most of these "mistakes" in nature produce no noticeable effects.[181] One in a million produce handicapped offspring that die young and their offspring die out. (Unfortunately, these accidents sometimes happen to human children.) However, one mutation of a gene in millions of mistakes produces a stronger offspring, one more suited for survival. This offspring begins a new branch in the tree of life—a new species of living things. And that is how this process of evolution—random mutation and natural selection—could have produced the millions of species of life on planet earth over millions of years, beginning with the first living cell and culminating in the selection of intelligent human beings who have discovered this wonderful process. It seemed like Darwin had discovered the Origin of Life and he believed that this origin did not require a Designer. In his theory, what looks like design is actually a random series of accidents underlying the evolution of living things. The origin of life seemed to be explained without God.

Darwin's evolution theory seems to work very well to explain the emergence of the millions of species of life from other species if the age of the earth is actually 4 billion years.[182] However, there is at least one gap in the theory—at least one unexplained leap in evolution—the transition from organic chemicals to the first living cell. This is a huge gap. Biologists have been attempting to duplicate this transition in the lab ever since Darwin's theory was published in 1859. That's more than 150 years of biochemical experimentation. The best they have been able to do in the lab is to synthesize many amino acids—building blocks of life—and other biochemicals.[183] They remain optimistic, but the origin of life remains elusive. Even some theistic scientists believe that the origin of life will be replicated in the lab and we should not continue to use this "gap" as evidence for God.[184] Nevertheless, the gap remains, and until an artificial cell is created in the lab, intelligent design and the Intelligent Designer are the best explanations we have for the existence of life.

The laws of thermodynamics are a stumbling block for evolution theory. Entropy, like Natural Selection, is a measure of "fitness" for survival. The second law of thermodynamics states that Entropy—a measure of chaos and disorder—is naturally and inexorably increasing—all things are gradually disintegrating into chaos and disorder. Entropy declares that the most stable situation, the one most "fit" to exist, in the closed universe is the most chaotic and disordered—the very opposite of the direction of evolution and natural selection. Evolution has been a phenomenal transition from random atoms to biochemicals to living cells to multicellular organisms and organs to plants, to fish, to birds and animals, to intelligent human beings—an amazing sequence of organization and complexification that goes in the opposite direction predicted by the law of entropy. Entropy predicts that—sooner or later—every complex system will disintegrate (will "die"). The most "fit" system of chemicals is a dead one. And so evolution should not have happened.

Robert Spitzer notes that the force of the universe toward maximum entropy / disorder is evidence that the universe cannot be eternal, cannot have always existed, that it has an origin (i.e., the Big Bang). If there were infinite time backward, entropy / disorder would have "maxed out" long ago—there would be no life, no order left in the universe that has had infinite time to evolve into the most "fit" energy state. No matter how large the universe is, this "closed system" of matter and energy would be a completely disordered state of maximum entropy long ago.[185] The fact that there exists today such an ordered and complex low-entropy portion of the universe on Planet Earth is evidence that it had a beginning—a Big Bang—just as it had been predicted by intelligent design-theories. According to Spitzer, Roger Penrose has even calculated the maximum entropy value of the universe, a state that should take billions of years to achieve.[186] But if the universe were eternal, maximum entropy (chaos) would have occurred billions of years ago. The same is true of the living cell—if living cells were eternal, they would have reached maximum entropy millions of years ago, and maximum entropy for the cell is death—there would be no living cells in the universe. So life and the universe had a beginning.

In some sense, the modern state of the science of life is something like my situation in the chemistry class at Notre Dame in 1966. I was faced with an explanation of the atom as having positively charged protons in the nucleus holding the electrons in their cloud and I failed to ask what was holding those like-charged protons together? The strong nuclear force. The strong nuclear force theory had not yet become widely known. It was not in Dr. Hoffman's textbook. Similarly, the science of life must ask itself, "What is holding those chemicals together in the cell? What is organizing those molecules into a living "machine" that fuels itself, moves itself, replicates itself, and eliminates wastes?" Paleontologist Priest Teilhard de Chardin offered a theory in 1955 in *The Phenomenon of Man*[187], but his book—which he intended to be "a scientific treatise"[188]—was dismissed by scientists as too mystical and metaphysical and by theologians as too unorthodox. Perhaps his terminology did not sound scientific enough for the scientists. Teilhard identified an energy field that he called the "within" of matter. All matter has a "without" and a "within".

> In the eyes of the physicist, nothing exists legitimately, at least up to now, except the *without* of things… it breaks down completely with man, in whom the existence of a *within* can no longer

be evaded, because it is the object of a direct intuition and the substance of all knowledge.[189]

Since the stuff of the universe has an inner aspect at one point of itself, there is necessarily *a double aspect to its structure*, that is to say in every region of space and time—in the same way, for instance, as it is granular: *coextensive with their Without, there is a Within to things*.[190]

The "within" of Teilhard could perhaps be more scientific sounding if we were to call it a "cell-field" or a "bio-field"—a "life force" that organizes the right organic chemicals into a living cell. This bio-field is a very low-energy one, difficult to measure, but it exerts sufficient pressure on the chemicals to make the living cell somehow more stable than its chemical constituents. The bio-field makes the highly organized and complex living cell somewhat more "fit" to survive than the inanimate chemical soup. There is a minute force in the bio-field that pushes lipids to form spherical shapes that are analogous to atoms, containing a nucleus and a spherical boundary surrounding the nucleus. The atom is a basic unit of matter—the cell is the basic unit of life. The atom has been split into its particles—the protons, neutrons and electrons. The cell (being large enough to be observed in the microscope) contains its sub-cellular structures—nucleus, cell membrane, mitochondria, ribosomes, proteins, genes, DNA and RNA, etc. All of these structures are composed of molecules of atoms—matter. But until these atoms are significantly organized into the complex equilibrium of a cell, there is no life at all. And it is the force of the bio-field, the "within" of matter, the "soul" that draws the chemicals into the complex organization, that animates the atoms and molecules and draws them into the delicate equilibrium of the cell.

Five forces of nature

So the "within" of matter—the bio-field—cell-field—produces the fifth force of nature, the "life-force" or "bio-force". The first field discovered was the gravitational field, operating primarily in the macro-realm of the universe, exerting an attractive force over huge distances and huge masses of atoms, like planets and stars and galaxies. The second field discovered was the electromagnetic field, operating primarily in the micro-realm of the atoms and molecules of atoms, exerting an attractive force over short distances between protons and electrons, positive and negative forces that attract each other and hold the atoms together. The third and fourth fields discovered were the strong and weak nuclear fields, operating in the nucleus of the atom, holding together the protons and neutrons that are contained in the nucleus, counteracting the repulsive forces on the like-charged protons (like electromagnetic charges repulse), preventing the nucleus of the atom from splitting apart. Finally, the fifth force field to be discovered is the bio-field, operating in the realm of the cell—a much smaller realm than that of gravity and a much larger realm than that of the atom-fields—attracting organic molecules into a delicate equilibrium of the cell, circling the lipid molecules into spheres creating cell membranes and nucleus membranes, each containing the liquid of life—the "cytoplasm" that provides the medium for animation of molecules. However, the fifth force field is a new discovery for scientists. The "within" of matter was already defined by Teilhard de Chardin in 1955, prior to the discoveries of the strong and weak forces of the nucleus of the atom in the 1960s. The "within" of matter is the bio-field. In fact, the bio-field is actually the first force field to be discovered—it was called the "soul" of the body. The "soul" is the "within" of matter, the bio-field of the cell. The "soul" was defined by the philosophers of metaphysics at least as long ago as Aristotle[191].

When the philosophers defined the soul, there was no modern science, no knowledge of the atom or the cell. The soul was the animator of living bodies—plants, animals and humans. So what is the connection between the within—the bio-field—and the soul? Teilhard de Chardin saw the soul as the product of the evolution from the cell. The soul is seen "as assuming the same granulation of matter itself… *Atomicity is a common property of the Within and the Without of things.*"[192] Teilhard saw the origin of the soul—and consciousness— in the first cell, perhaps even in the first particle of matter. Animation and consciousness may be found in their most elemental forms in the particles of matter. As matter evolved from the most elemental particles into one-celled forms of life into multi-celled plants, animals and humans, the "within" evolved along with the "without" of matter according to "the great Law of complexity and consciousness" to explain "first of all the invisibility, then the appearance, and then the gradual dominance of the *within* in comparison to the *without* of things."[193] Counterbalancing the force of increasing entropy (chaos and disorder), there is a force in nature toward increasing order, complexity and organization. There is a delicate balance—a delicate equilibrium—attracting molecules into a complex organization of a living cell. The force that counteracts entropy—the force of the bio-field, the "within" of matter—powers evolution toward greater and greater complexity, organization and order—toward higher animals and humans—and the "within" of matter evolves along with matter. As the "within" becomes complex and organized, it increasingly resembles the "soul", the "within", the bio-field of the human person—including consciousness as we experience it. The law of entropy is counterbalanced by the bio-field that produces "the coiling up of the molecule upon itself"[194] and organizes its components into a living cell. Mother Nature has a soul-force. Mother Nature has been designed—programmed—to produce and nurture life. And this design requires an Intelligent Designer—God.

The first cell was a fragile equilibrium of complex chemicals, bonds and the bio-field. And according to the law of entropy, the first cell eventually died, as all "machines" do—the law of entropy states that there are no perpetual motion machines. All order sooner or later ends in disorder/death. Except for one thing—the cell has the power to reproduce itself about 50 times before it dies.[195] Reproduction is one key form of cellular activity—one key sign of life. And though the parent cell eventually died, its offspring were able to continue the evolution of life. And once life emerged from the "primordial soup" of chemicals, it has been able to survive perhaps 3 billion years to today. And all the cells produced from the first cell would be identical to the first cell, except for a second thing—the genetic code does not copy itself perfectly. The process of copying the genetic code of the cell rarely, but sometimes, makes "mistakes". When the copying process makes a "mistake", it produces a mutation in the new cell—the new cell is no longer an identical twin of the parent cell. The new cell is different. And most of the time, there is no evident consequence. But sometimes, "different" is problematic. The original cell was a delicate equilibrium of a living, amazingly organized and complex bunch of chemicals animated by the bio-field and bio-forces—its delicate state means that it could easily die with the slightest alteration of the equilibrium. Life generally does not like change because change can mean death. The bio-field produces a very slight bio-force, much more delicate than the other forces of nature. Most mutations of the genes "have little or no consequence".[196] Some produce an offspring that is still born or one that dies out very quickly—it does not reproduce itself. But one mutation in a million "wins the lottery"—its mutation actually made the new cell stronger than the parent cell. Perhaps the new mutation added a flagellum—a tail—to the cell, giving the new cell locomotion that the parent cell did not have, making the mutation more "fit" to survive than its parent. So the mutation was selected by "natural selection" to survive and reproduce itself about 50 times. This mutation actually "won the lottery" twice—once when the gene-copying made a "mistake"—happening perhaps one in a million times—and secondly, when the "mistake" turned out to be naturally selected to reproduce—another one-in-a-million lottery. Mother Nature has apparently nurtured this evolutionary process for perhaps 3 billion years, producing the millions of species of living plants and animals and humans that inhabit Mother Earth.

Three arguments for God—Anthropy, Entropy and DNA

What we have uncovered so far are two new versions of the classical "teleological argument" for the existence of God. St. Thomas Aquinas "argued that unintelligent objects cannot be ordered unless they are done so by an intelligent being, which means that there must be an intelligent being to move objects toward their ends: God."[197] What we have proposed here are two new arguments for the existence of a Super-Intelligence behind the order of the universe. Modern science has added a significant amount of evidence confirming the ancient "teleological argument" of St. Thomas Aquinas in the 13th century—his argument predicted that we would discover even greater complexity and order in the universe because it has been designed by an Intelligent Designer. That is what has happened. What are the two new arguments for design? They are the argument from Anthropy and the argument from Entropy.

We have been exploring above the arguments from Anthropy and Entropy. Anthropy refers to that extremely improbable set of forces and constants that must have been programmed by a Programmer to produce and nurture life. Entropy refers to the second law of thermodynamics that states that Entropy / disorder naturally and inevitably increases with time. But evolution in general and the emergence of the first living cell go against Entropy—order and complexity (and design) have been increasing (meaning that Entropy /disorder is decreasing, contrary to the second law of thermodynamics). Increasing design, order and complexity all point to a Designer—God. Now we proceed to a third argument for God—the DNA argument.

The DNA argument for God is another modern version of St. Thomas Aquinas' "teleological argument". We have reviewed the evolutionary process above and we highlighted the role of reproduction and genetics in that process. Replication of genes in cell division is key to reproduction and evolution. We have seen how accuracy in the replication of genes is very important and highly probable—there are very few "mistakes" in the process. And the occasional "mistakes" in gene replication are essential to evolution theory—without occasional "mistakes" in gene replication, there would have been no mutations and no new steps in the evolution process—it was the occasional "mistake" in gene replication that created a rare new species in the evolutionary time-line, eventually enabling the evolution of consciousness and the human species. That is why "mistake" is in quotation marks—what looks like a mistake is actually part of the design in evolution. This is the process that also accidentally produces mutations ("mistakes") that can sometimes cause genetic illnesses or malformations that severely handicap or cause premature births and deaths. They are accidents of nature rather than choices made by God. These can cause Jobe Syndrome, leading us to question "why?" The answer to "why" is the dynamic of mutation and natural selection. These are the "tools" of evolution. That is the wonderful process of creation. Often we are sad for the "mistakes" but thank Mother Nature for the mutations that eventually created us. Without them we humans would never have evolved. But the secret hidden in this process was only recently discovered in the 1950s—De-oxy-ribo- Nucleic Acid—DNA. DNA has been called *The Language of God*[198] and *The Signature in the Cell*.[199] The first title comes from the book by Francis Collins who led the team of scientists who mapped the sequence of millions of bases in human DNA in 2003. The second title comes from the book by Stephen Meyer in which he argues for the existence of a Super-Intelligence hidden behind the DNA codes. Indeed, Meyer's book shows the evidence that the Intelligent Designer uses DNA as a language to create and sustain and reproduce life.

DNA—The Language of God

Remember the moon landing story? We imagined the Russians landing on the moon and finding a moon-rover or a laptop computer. It is like the archeologist who discovers arrowheads, pottery and tools at a dig-site. She knows that humans had been there. Cave drawings are even stronger evidence for intelligent life—they are a form of hieroglyphics—telling a story by means of pictures. Hieroglyphics is a language. It took archeologists about 2000 years to decipher the Egyptian version of hieroglyphics. In fact, they never deciphered it. They discovered the Rosetta stone, a giant stone with one decree of Pharaoh engraved in three languages, including hieroglyphics and Greek. This enabled them to translate the other languages from the Greek which was well known.[200] They knew hieroglyphics was a language—they just couldn't decipher it. (See Image 8.)

Image 8: The Rosetta Stone

Similarly, only recently have marine biologists deciphered some of the primitive "language" of the Dolphin.[201] When the archeologists discover a language, they know that intelligent life has been there—primitive intelligence in the case of the Dolphin and advanced intelligence in the case of the Egyptian hieroglyphics. So too in our story, if the Russians found a laptop on the moon, they would know that it was tool, a product of intelligent life having been there. But they could not be sure that they were discovering a language in that tool. However, when their computer experts powered it up and analyzed the electronic contents, they discovered that it used the same binary digital language that their computers used—they were able to translate the computer code into

Russian. They knew for certain that very intelligent beings were there—probably American humans because of the language and because the Americans had advanced technology capable of space travel. But what if, instead of a laptop, they found a living green plant on the moon? Inside a huge bubble half full of water and half full of air, with large green leaves in the air and roots in the water? This microcosm of air, water, balloon and plant seemed to be a living system in equilibrium. Amazing how it could survive on the moon. But what is more amazing is what they would have discovered in the lab analysis of a tiny piece of the plant—they would have found DNA. DNA is the key to all living things that we know of—it is a huge macromolecule that serves as a blueprint for the construction of millions of various proteins required for the construction of cells of all kinds. DNA is a language similar to computer language—not binary and digital with two numbers, one and zero, but with four letters corresponding to the four bases in the DNA chain of macromolecules[202]. The four letters in the DNA alphabet in their various sequences are not randomly positioned—they are in a precise formation to form "words" and "sentences" and "books". In fact, a team of scientists headed by Francis Collins decoded the whole sequence of letters in the DNA of the human genome in 2003. The "book" of the structure of human DNA contained "3 billion letters of the DNA code".[203] (In contrast, my book contains about 250,000 letters.) Collins called the DNA code "this most powerful textbook of medicine"[204] and "the language of God". "This book was written in the DNA language by which God spoke life into being".[205] If DNA is truly a language, then the Russian astronauts in our story would have discovered evidence of a Super-Intelligent Designer, a person whose intelligence far surpasses human intelligence, a programmer who has programmed billions of letters in the nucleus of each plant cell. Our programmer has essentially written the manufacturer's manual for the construction of every cell (there are 100 trillion cells in the human body[206]). That is the largest book ever written. Our Designer is so intelligent.

I can't proceed with our discussion of DNA without mentioning a key religious person involved in the background of the Watson and Crick discovery of the double-helix structure of DNA. Sister Miriam Stimson (1913-2002) was an Adrian Dominican nun, a chemist and a professor at a small college in Adrian, Michigan, now known as Siena Heights University. "She had a role in the history of understanding DNA."[207] The details of her role in this history have been documented by Jun Tsuji, associate professor of Biology at Siena Heights University, in his book, *The Soul of DNA*.[208] The field of analytical chemistry did not include many women in the 1950s—Miriam was often the only woman presenting at conferences.[209] "Catholic sisters, like Miriam, were among the first American feminists".[210] Miriam was only the second woman (after Madame Marie Curie) to be invited to speak at the Sorbonne in Paris.[211] Her key contribution to the discovery of the structure of DNA was her invention of the "pressed disc" made from Potassium Bromide (KBr) which proved to be a superior medium for the recording of the infrared spectra of the DNA bases, confirming their structure.[212] She offers us a significant model for women and for religious persons in the field of science. Sister Miriam Stimson is another significant theist—scientist.

Stephen Meyer published what may be the first and only peer-reviewed scientific paper arguing for Intelligent Design from the evidence of DNA. His article was entitled "The origin of biological information and the higher taxonomic categories." It appeared in Volume 117, number 2 (August 2004) issue of the *Proceedings of the Biological Society of Washington*.[213] The article produced a storm of controversy in both the scientific and popular media.[214] Stephen Meyer's book, *Signature in the Cell*, is an extensive elaboration on the argument for Intelligent Design from the evidence of DNA. Meyer makes the claim that this is a legitimate scientific theory, not a religious one, and he clearly distinguishes Intelligent Design theory from Biblical Creationism:

> The [Intelligent Design] (ID) theory does not challenge the idea of evolution defined as change over time or even common ancestry, but it does dispute the Darwinian idea that the cause of all biological change is wholly blind and undirected. Even so, the theory is not based on biblical doctrine. Intelligent design is an inference from scientific evidence, not a deduction from religious authority.[215]

Meyer credits biochemist Michael Behe and his book, *Darwin's Black Box*, with "almost single-handedly" putting "the idea of intelligent design on the cultural and scientific map".[216] And many other scientists admit they are dumfounded by the DNA evidence. Meyer highlighted the three who wrote the book, *The Mystery of Life's Origin*.

> Three of the scientists on the panel had just published a controversial book called *The Mystery of Life's Origin* with the prominent

New York publisher of scientific monographs. Their book provided a comprehensive critique of the attempts that had been made to explain how the first life had arisen from the primordial ocean, the so-called pre-biotic soup. These scientists, Charles Thaxton, Walter Bradley, and Roger Olson, had come to the conclusion that all such theories had failed to explain the origin of the first life. Surprisingly, the other scientists on the panel – all experts in the field – did not dispute this critique. What the other scientists did dispute was a controversial new hypothesis that Thaxton and his colleagues had floated in the epilogue of their book in an attempt to explain the DNA enigma. They have suggested that the information in DNA might have originated from an intelligent source or, as they put it, an "intelligent cause."... "Special Creation by a Creator beyond the cosmos is a plausible view of origin science." The code, in other words, pointed to a programmer.[217]

DNA is a language containing an alphabet of four letters, communicating a message in every cell of a body in digital-like code, providing a blueprint and assembly instructions for every cell in the body—a veritable manufacturer's manual for living things. The discovery of DNA has brought biology into the "information age".

In Darwin's time few, if any, biologists talked about biological or genetic information, but today they routinely refer to DNA, RNA, and proteins as carriers or repositories of information. Biologists tell us that DNA stores and transmits "genetic information," that it expresses the "genetic message," that it stores "assembly instructions," a "genetic blueprint," or "digital code." Biology has entered its own information age, and scientists seeking to explain the origin of life have taken note. Life does not consist of just matter and energy, but also information.[218]

The DNA code is not only information—it also directs the information to be used in the cell in the manufacturing process of proteins of all kinds.

... DNA also contains information in the sense of Webster's second definition: it contains "alternative sequences or arrangements of something that produce a specific effect."... DNA displays a property – functional specificity – that transcends the merely mathematical formalism of Shannon's theory.[219]

Is this significant? In fact, it is profoundly mysterious. Apart from the molecules comprising the gene expression system and machinery of the cell, sequences or structures exhibiting such specified complexity or specified information are not found anywhere in the natural – that is, the nonhuman - world... Software and its encoded sequences of digital characters function in a way that most closely parallels the base sequences in DNA. Thus, oddly, at nearly the same time that computer scientists were beginning to develop machine languages, molecular biologists were discovering that living cells had been using something akin to machine code or software all along... How did these digitally encoded and specifically sequenced instructions in DNA arise?[220]

The computer code programmed in every cell points to a Programmer.

Meyer recalled his encounter with Fred Hoyle at Cambridge. "Famous for his pioneering work on the fine-tuning problem in physics and cosmology," he was visiting there "to explain why he had come to reject chemical evolution theory".

Afterward I asked him directly about whether he thought the information stored in DNA might point to an intelligent source. His eyes brightened, and he motioned to me to continue walking with him after his lecture. "That would certainly make life a lot easier to explain," he said.[221]

The atheistic scientists are determined to explain the origin of DNA as the result of random biochemical interactions rather than the "language of God". As it turns out, the odds of producing DNA by chance are as astronomically low as the odds for the anthropic universe.

The simplest extant cell, *Mycoplasma genitalium*—a tiny bacterium that inhabits the human urinary tract—requires "only" 482 proteins to perform its necessary functions and 562,000 bases of DNA (just under 1,200 base pairs per gene) to assemble those proteins.[222]

...the relevant probability calculation can be made by either analyzing the odds of arranging amino acids into a functional protein or by analyzing the odds of arranging nucleotide bases into a gene that encodes that protein. Because it turns out to be simpler to make the calculation using proteins, that's what most origin-of-life scientists have done.[223]

For every combination of amino acids that produce a functional protein there exists a vast number of other possible combinations that do not... even a relatively short protein of, say, 150 amino acids represent one sequence among an astronomically large number of other possible sequence combinations (approximately 10 to the 195th power).[224]

That number is equal to 1 followed by 195 zeros!!! This protein has won the lottery many times! The total number of atoms in our galaxy is "only" the number 1 followed by 65 zeros.[225]

Believe it or not, the odds of finding [one] marked atom in our galaxy are markedly better (about a billion times better) than those of finding a functional protein among all the sequences of corresponding length.[226]

Another way of describing the odds is "less than one chance in a trillion trillion". [227] These kinds of odds would require nearly infinite time and more than a trillion trillion attempts in order to win this lottery, in order to find one marked atom in our galaxy. It makes more sense to conclude that DNA is a language communicating building instructions from a super-intelligent Designer and Builder of the universe.

Physical chemist and philosopher of science, Michael Polanyi, had a significant influence on Stephen Meyer. Polanyi argued that DNA is a language that cannot be reduced to physical and chemical laws.[228] Stephen Meyer's main point is that "Life does not consist of just matter and energy, but also information".[229] DNA is the "signature in the cell" written by a super-intelligent Author of Life.

CHAPTER 6

Predictions from the Intelligent Design Hypothesis

(Note to the reader: Chapter six attempts to translate some of the language of science and natural law into common language. If you get bogged down in this language, please proceed to chapter 7, Sister Water (page 117).)

Stephen Meyer agrees with the generally held belief that a scientific hypothesis requires "positive evidence for the efficacy" of the hypothesis and "refutations of other relevant causal hypotheses using either predictive methods of testing, evaluations of explanatory power, or both".[230] Predictions can be both positive and negative—evidence in the lab for the hypothesis and/or evidence in the lab that alternative hypotheses do not explain the data well. He highlighted the work of microbiologist Douglas Axe who "devised a way to test this ID-inspired prediction" "that mutation and selection lack the capacity to produce fundamentally new genes and proteins".[231] [ID = Intelligent Design]. Meyer goes on to outline "a dozen ID-inspired predictions"[232] Most of these predictions are too technical to be understood by non-scientists.

However, one example that may be translatable into common language is the prediction that studies of what appear to be bad designs in nature—such as "virulent bacteria" that cause terrible diseases like ebola—"should reveal either a) reasons for the designs that show a hidden functional logic or b) evidence of decay of originally good designs".[233] In other words, studies should discover that a terrible virus or bacterium has a functional purpose in living systems or that its genetic structure deteriorated from a "good" virus or bacterium into a "bad" one. One example that comes to mind that is already widely known is the e-coli bacterium—in the colon, it has a digestive function, whereas in contaminated food it is poisonous. We have discovered a functional purpose for an otherwise diabolical life form.[234]

Some predictions from Intelligent Design theory have either already been proven true in the in the lab or are testable in the lab. Perhaps the most noteworthy is the Big Bang itself. Competing theories of the origin of the universe were debated for centuries—was there an origin of the universe or not? Perhaps the majority of scientists have believed in the eternal universe—that matter, and more recently, matter and energy, are constant—they were neither created nor can they be destroyed. Metaphysicians tended to believe in a beginning to the universe—that there had to be an "uncaused cause" and an "unmoved mover" in the beginning.[235] And neither side of the argument believed that there would ever be a way to test these two hypotheses in the lab—how could we test an event that occurred thousands or billions of years ago—or an event that never occurred? Both scientists and philosophers believed that the choice between these hypotheses was a matter of faith and metaphysics, not of physics. Both sides were wrong—the "red shift" was measured in the radiation of the stars and planets, showing clear evidence that the "Big Bang" occurred and that it was datable—13.8 billion years ago.[236] Intelligent Design theory fits the Big Bang scenario and the eternal universe theory does not. At this moment in history, even the Bible claim fits the data better than the materialists' claim. Laboratory data has confirmed that our universe had a beginning point. Scientists like Stephen Hawking and many others are determined to restore the eternal universe theory by means of "The Grand Design" theory, but he acknowledges that "the original hope of physicists to produce a single theory... may have to be abandoned."[237]

Then there is the prediction that studies of chemical evolution in the lab will continue to fail to produce a living cell. This is one of the "gaps" in scientific knowledge that continues to elude explanation. Intelligent Design theory could explain the "jump" from organic chemicals to cells—the Designer could have created the bio-field that animated the first cell and the DNA code that directed the assembly of proteins that structured the first cell. Alternative theories of "spontaneous generation" from a "pre-biotic soup" of chemicals so far have not been confirmed in the lab. Intelligent Design theory predicts that the results of these lab efforts will continue to be negative.[238]

The hypothesis of cell forces and a cell-field—or bio-field—may be measurable. This fifth force would be very slight and difficult to measure but the sophistication of our measurement tools continues to increase. It may be measurable in the form of entropy—entropy (disorder) could show at least a slight increase at the point of death in any animal or human. The bio-force toward order and organization leaves the body at the moment of death.

The Prediction of the "Noosphere" and the "Internet"

Teilhard de Chardin called the cell-field the "within" of matter.[239] This makes him the father of the cell-field hypothesis. He is also the inventor of the definition of evolution as "the continual growth of this 'psychic' or 'radial' energy" and "deepening of consciousness".[240] Evolution has a direction toward increased complexity and consciousness.

> ...evolution has a precise *orientation* and a privileged *axis*...I believe I can see a direction and a line of progress for life, a line and a direction which are in fact so well marked that I am convinced their reality will be universally admitted by the science of tomorrow.[241]

Teilhard is predicting that the direction of evolution toward consciousness will become increasingly recognized by the science of our time. We cannot escape the reality of our own consciousness—our own "within".

> We have merely to look into ourselves to perceive it—the nervous system. We are in a positive way aware of one single 'interiority' in the world: our own directly, and at the same time that of other men by immediate equivalence, thanks to language.[242]

Interestingly, this direction in evolution toward consciousness doesn't end with the human individuals. Teilhard de Chardin proposed a theory that evolution is continuing beyond the birth of consciousness in individuals and groups, and even beyond the evolution of cultures. The next step in evolution is the emergence of the "noosphere"—"noogenesis"—thought and consciousness now surround the globe.

> The biological change of state terminating in the awakening of thought does not represent merely a critical point that the individual or even the species must pass through. Vaster than that, it affects life in its organic totality, and consequently, it marks a transformation affecting the state of the entire planet… We saw geogenesis promoted to biogenesis, which turned out in the end to be nothing else than psychogenesis…the next term in the series manifests itself. Psychogenesis has led to man. Now it effaces itself… and a higher function— the engendering and subsequent development of the mind, in one word, noogenesis.[243]

> A new era in evolution, the era of noogenesis… The fire spreads in ever widening circles till finally the whole planet is covered… it is really a new layer, the 'thinking layer'… In other words, outside and above the biosphere there is the noosphere… we have the beginning of a new age. The earth 'gets a new skin'. Better still, it finds its soul.[244]

Teilhard's theory looked into the future to predict this layer of intelligence and communication surrounding earth and transforming planet earth into a new living and conscious being. Teilhard did not restrict this new layer of consciousness surrounding planet earth to the expansion of human population and geography. He foresaw the use of electromagnetic waves as a powerful tool of communication for the planet. Teilhard predicted the advent of something like the internet 40 years before its invention.

> Better still: thanks to the prodigious biological event represented by the discovery of electro-magnetic waves, each individual finds himself henceforth (actively and passively) simultaneously present, over land and sea, in every corner of the earth.[245]

How did he know that electromagnetic waves could enable us to be "simultaneously present" over the whole of Mother Earth? In his time he knew of TV and radio. But this is bigger—internet and satellite. The whole planet is connected in real time. Teilhard predicted something like the internet in 1948 (or earlier).

Predictions from natural moral law—the 4th Proof for the Existence of God

Perhaps the vast majority of predictions based on Intelligent Design theory are moral ones. The theory claims that moral laws are built into the universe just like the laws of physics. This is the 4th proof for the existence of God. There is no room for "relativism" in ethics or physics. The outcomes of human behavior according to (or in violation of) the natural moral laws can be—and have been—tested by the statistical tools of sociology. The bulk of these predictions will be included in chapter ten on Mortal Sin and the Second Death. In this section, I will restrict the predictions to four:

- Without the Intelligent Benevolent Designer, there is no foundation for morality. Societies based on atheism will produce unprecedented levels of disrespect for human life, involving the killing of millions.
- Devoted believers in the Benevolent Intelligent Designer will demonstrate unprecedented levels of altruism / unselfishness.
- Religious people will give more money to charity than non-religious people.
- Religious people will be healthier and live longer than non-religious people.

Religion is as ancient as human beings. Belief in the Great Spirit and lesser spirits is evident in most human cultures. Some ancient religious cultures were as diabolical as some of our modern cultures (e.g., involving human sacrifices and child sacrifices to their god(s))[246]. But cultural evolution (the natural selection of the most "fit" cultures) has virtually eliminated the most diabolical religions by way of human selection of the great world religions (analogous to natural selection of genetic mutations). The majority of the population of the world believes in one of six great religions (Christianity, Islam, Hinduism, Buddhism, Taoism, Judaism).[247] The French Revolution of the 18th century produced perhaps the first atheistic government that we know of. But it was the 19th century that produced the most famous atheist thinkers like Friedrich

Nietzsche[248] ("God is dead"[249]), Karl Marx[250] (atheistic communism: "[Religion] is the opium of the people"[251]), Sigmund Freud[252] (atheistic psychology: "The future of an Illusion" [religion]"[253]) and Charles Darwin (evolution theorist explaining living species without an act of God). Thinkers like these influenced the 20th century leaders of atheistic and anti-religious regimes that produced the massive persecution of religions as well as genocide, eugenics[254] and political persecution on a grand scale. There were more people executed by their own countrymen during World War II and its aftermath than there were killed in combat. Adolf Hitler[255] is estimated to have killed 6 million Jews and at least 6 million other "enemies of the regime" and undesirables. "The number of civilians killed during the Second World War was unprecedented in warfare; the casualties constituted the deadliest conflict in human history."[256] Hitler may not have been anti-religion or anti-Christian, but he knew that the Church in Germany was an obstacle in the way of his movement and if intimidation did not silence her, mass executions would. Perhaps the icon of the persecuted Catholics was Father Maximillian Kolbe, a Polish priest incarcerated at Auschwitz as an enemy of the regime and who volunteered to be executed in the place of a condemned Jewish man.[257] Josef Stalin[258] is estimated to have killed between 4 million and 10 million non-combatants among his own countrymen in his political purge in the Soviet Union.[259] His communism followed the pattern set by Karl Marx that included overt atheism. Likewise, for communist dictator Mao Zedong[260]. His leadership of the communist revolution in China led to the largest atheistic culture in the world and to an estimated 4 million to 10 million executions of civilian countrymen during his political purge. His was "the top incidence of excess mortality in human history".[261] These regimes offer evidence for our claim that without admitting a Supreme Intelligent Designer, humans make themselves gods and morality reverts to "the survival of the fittest" and "might makes right" and an absence of altruism. Natural Law proponents predicted the bloodbaths of the 20th century.[262] Dostoevsky stated it most profoundly: "If God does not exist, everything is permitted."[263]

The second noteworthy moral prediction of Intelligent Design theory is that devoted believers in the Benevolent Intelligent Designer will demonstrate unprecedented levels of altruism / unselfishness. We mentioned above the name of Maximillian Kolbe. He is not only the icon of persecuted Catholics during the Holocaust, he is also the icon of believers in the Supreme Intelligent and Benevolent Designer and of altruistic love of the neighbor—Father Kolbe volunteered to take the place of a condemned Jewish man at Auschwitz. And for this sacrifice, Kolbe was declared a "Martyr of charity" and "The Patron Saint of Our Difficult Century".[264] Alongside Father Kolbe there are hundreds of declared saints who have been models of unselfishness. Most of these saints have been professional religious men and women who have taken the vows of Poverty, Celibacy and Obedience. In making these vows, these men and women gave their wealth and possessions to the poor, gave up their rights to marry and have children, and submitted to the will of their superiors in the religious orders. These hundreds of religious men and women by their unselfishness imitated the altruism of their God and their Savior. Their Intelligent Designer is also a Benevolent Designer whose Love for people is demonstrated by the act of creation—the Supreme Intelligence decided to share existence with creatures—a supreme act of altruism. We should not be surprised that most people, including believers, act selfishly in accord with the theory of natural selection (i.e., they succumb to the consequences of "original sin"). Selfishness is programmed into the evolution process. Rather, we should be surprised that anyone could overcome the force of natural selfishness to act in a clearly supernatural, unselfish way. We should be surprised that St. Catherine of Siena volunteered to nurse people during the Black Plague,[265] or that St. Francis kissed a leper,[266] or that Father Damian chose to live with lepers[267] or that Mother Teresa gave up her comfortable convent to become a servant to "the poorest of the poor", or that members of religious orders do not get paychecks (all their checks are made out to the religious order, not to the individual). In fact, we should be surprised that there could exist for centuries religious orders who successfully practice voluntary "communism" while coerced communism has failed in the Soviet Union. Communism fails without God. Communism is possible with God. (Acts 2:43-47 and Acts 4:32-37) Benevolent Design believers have shown evidence that supernatural altruism can exist in a selfish world.

The third moral prediction is that religious people will give more money to charity than non-religious people. This prediction has been studied for years by Arthur Brooks, a Syracuse University Professor of Citizenship and Public Affairs. The fruit of his research is his book, *Who Really Cares? America's Charity Divide—Who Gives, Who Doesn't and Why It Matters*.[268] Brooks began his research with an admission of his political bias:

> When I started doing research on charity, I
> expected to find that political liberals—who, I

believed, generally *cared* more about others than conservatives did—would turn out to be the most privately charitable people. So when my early findings led to the opposite conclusion, I assumed I had made some sort of technical error. I re-ran analyses. I got new data. Nothing worked. In the end, I had no option except to change my views.

I confess my prejudices of the past here to emphasize that the findings in this book—many of which may appear conservative and support a religious, hardworking, family oriented lifestyle—are faithful to the best available evidence, and contrary to my political and cultural roots. Indeed, the irresistible pull of empirical evidence in this book is what changed the way I see the world.[269]

Contrary to his political bias, Brooks was compelled by the data to change his world view and to conclude that religious people not only give more money to charity but they also volunteer more time as well.

In 2000, 81 percent of one large nationwide survey of Americans said they gave money to charity, and 57 percent said they volunteered. But the likelihood of giving and volunteering was dramatically different between religious people and secularists: Religious people were 25 percentage points more likely to give than secularists (91 to 66 percent). Religious

people were also 23 points more likely to volunteer (67 to 44 percent)... in 2000, religious
people—who, per family earned exactly the
same amount as secular people, $49,000—
gave about 3.5 times more money per year (an
average of $2,210 vs. $642). They also volunteered more than twice as often (12 times per
year vs. 5.8 times).[270]

Arthur Brooks has done the empirical research that confirms
the prediction that people who believe in the Intelligent and
Benevolent Designer will give more money to charity. It is a
more specific application of the theory described in the first
and second moral predictions—without a Supreme Intelligent
Designer there is no foundation for morality—I am my own
God. Whereas, if I acknowledge a Supreme Intelligent and
Benevolent Designer, I am safe and secure in the universe—
the Supreme Force in the universe "has my back"—I don't
need to be selfish.

The fourth moral prediction of Intelligent Design theory is
that religious people will be healthier and live longer than
non-religious people. If the laws of nature include moral laws,
and if they were designed by an Intelligent and Benevolent
Designer, then the devotion to the Designer should produce
better compliance with moral laws—and better compliance
with natural moral laws should produce healthier outcomes
for the practitioners. This kind of hypothesis is indeed testable by means of statistical analysis of longitudinal studies
of believers and non-believers. The prediction is that the
believers will have better health outcomes. This is the primary finding in the vast majority of the 1600 statistical studies

in The *Handbook of Religion and Health*, edited by the medical team of Koenig, McCullough, and Larson.[271] This kind of finding that "religion is good for your health" should be information readily available to patients in medical clinics along with all the other wellness information provided.[272] Image 9 shows one of the most important studies in the *Handbook of Religion and Health* [273] on longevity:

Image 9:

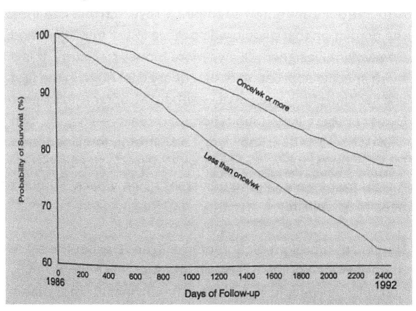

Image 9 charts a longitudinal study of 3,968 senior citizens (age 65 years or over) from 1986 to 1992. The vertical coordinate is the percentage of the 3,968 who are still alive at each point. The horizontal coordinate is the number of days (or years) of the study. In 1986, the whole sample was alive (100 %). The upper line shows the percentages of the sample who were frequent church attenders (once a week or more);

the lower line shows the number of less frequent church attenders (less than once a week). At the end of the 6 years of the study, 77% of the frequent attenders were still alive, whereas 63% of the less frequent attenders were alive. "The relative hazard of dying was reduced by 46% for frequent attenders… equivalent to [the effect] of abstaining from cigarette smoking."[274]

Conclusions

We have reviewed a sampling of some of the most important predictions based on the theory of Intelligent Design of natural law. The scientific method always involves the testing of theories by means of predictions based on the theories and studies based on the predictions. As we have seen above, most of these predictions have already been studied and so far, the outcomes of Intelligent Design (ID) theory predictions have supported the theory. This kind of information should qualify Intelligent Design theory as a scientific proposal inviting further testing and studying. The current status of the ID theory is the publication of the single peer-reviewed scientific article by Stephen Meyer in the *Proceedings of the Biological Society of Washington, D.C..*[275] Many scientists were scandalized by the publication of the article, attempting to censor and cover-up ID theory, but many other scientists want to include the theory in the scientific debate.[276] Censorship is an unscientific response to ID theory. Mother Earth is designed by the Intelligent Designer, programmed for the creation and nurturing of life in general and intelligent life in particular. Programming presumes the existence of a Programmer. Mother Earth is animated by an Intelligent and Benevolent Designer. Anthropy, Entropy, the

DNA language and Natural Law all point to the Intelligent Designer of Mother Earth as the Programmer. Even evolution theory itself demands some explanation for the giant leap from organic chemicals to the first cell and the reversal of the "entropy arrow" involved.[277] And evolution theory also demands some explanation for the mysterious language of DNA programmed in the cell. Even atheist Richard Dawkins admits that there is currently no explanation for the origin of the first cell. In his interview with Ben Stein, Dawkins resorts to metaphysics by expressing his faith in the possibility that an alien brought one living cell through space attached to a crystal which landed on Mother Earth and which began the evolution process here.[278] "Francis Crick (who… discovered the DNA double helix), [also proposed] that life forms must have arrived on Earth from outer space".[279] It seems like the atheist-scientists have a more fantastic mythology than the great world religions.

Sister Water, Brothers Wind, Air and Fire

(Note to the reader: Chapter seven attempts to translate some of the language of biology and chemistry into common language. If you get bogged down in this language, please proceed to Chapter 8, Brother Pain (page 131).)

The ancients believed that there were four elements in the universe—earth, air, fire and water.[280] And so St. Francis borrowed these elements from the science of his time to construct his hymn of praise for creation (chapter four). We have seen in chapter 5 how Mother Earth is the origin and nurturer of life and how she must be animated by the Intelligent and Benevolent Designer. In this chapter, we examine the other elements—air, water and fire—and how they point to an Intelligent Designer.

Humans cannot live without air for more than a few minutes. Humans cannot live without water for more than a few days. Humans cannot live without food for more than a few weeks.[281] Fortunately for us, Mother Earth happens to have an atmosphere composed of air, water and food-atoms. Air is composed (approximately 78%) of Nitrogen (a food atom), 21% of Oxygen (the key atom for breathing and respiration) and 1% of water vapor.[282] Many of us are shocked that Carbon Dioxide (blamed for "global warming") is not on the list of ingredients of Brother Air. The three ingredients above account for (almost) 100% of the atmosphere. Where is the "carbon footprint"? It is there. Carbon dioxide accounts for 0.04 % of the atmosphere. Why is this significant? We have seen above (in chapter 4) how amazingly improbable it is to have an anthropic (human-friendly) universe. We have seen above (in chapter 5) how amazingly improbable it was to have an anthropic Mother Earth. What does this mean? It means that we won the lottery when it came to the perfect spacing of Mother Earth from Brother Sun—the perfect distance to have a significant tropical zone and temperate zone—perfect temperatures for the creation and nurturing of life. But we actually won the lottery twice—if millions of planets exist in the universe with the right temperatures for nurturing life—there are also millions of these planets that do not have the perfect balance of atoms and molecules in the atmosphere surrounding them—indeed, some of them do not have an atmosphere at all![283] So we won the lottery by being on Mother Earth with temperate temperatures—and we won the lottery again by being able to breath Brother Air surrounding Mother Earth. Both of these qualities qualify Mother Earth to be Anthropic (human life-friendly) and both of these qualities make Mother Earth amazingly improbable. Why are we so lucky to have won the planet lottery twice? Why did our bodies' chemicals end up in this extremely rare corner of the giant universe? Only the Intelligent Designer knows the answer to these questions.

What makes Mother Earth's atmosphere so perfect for life? Because of the wonderful, delicate balance of chemicals in it. The very delicate structure of the first living cell required a balance of Oxygen, Nitrogen, Carbon Dioxide and Water—the same balance that we require as humans. In order to know how delicate is this balance, consider the "global warming" theory and the "greenhouse effect" of Carbon Dioxide.[284] Carbon Dioxide is being blamed for causing the greenhouse effect and global warming—yet it is less than 1% of the earth's atmosphere. How a slight change in 0.04% of the atmosphere could produce such a catastrophic prediction of negative global effects is amazing, and it highlights the delicacy of the balance of chemicals in the air. None of the ancients knew of these chemicals nor the delicacy of the balance of them. They only knew that Brother Air was essential for life.

Carbon-Fixing

Why is the balance of chemicals in the earth's atmosphere so delicate and critical? Global warming is only the most recent chapter of the story. It took modern science to discover the amazing reasons for the chemical balance and the discovery of atoms and molecules and cells to appreciate how anthropic (human-friendly) our atmosphere is. The ancients could not have known this. Now we know that Carbon atoms are the primary fuel of living things. But carbon in the form of carbon dioxide (0.04% of air) is poisonous to us—we excrete carbon-dioxide because it is a "waste-product" of respiration and if we tighten a plastic bag over our head, we will suffocate within a few minutes. We cannot consume carbon in the form of carbon-dioxide. So where is the Intelligent Designer of this planet? Did the Intelligent Designer make a mistake or is the

Designer Malevolent rather than Benevolent—an evil force rather than a caring force? Intelligent Design theory would predict that the Intelligent Designer is Benevolent and neither made a mistake nor wants to destroy life. Instead, the Intelligent Designer designed the green plants before animals in the evolutionary sequence of events because the green plants can consume carbon dioxide. The DNA of plant cells assembled an amazing cellular process called "photosynthesis".[285] Photosynthesis takes place in the green chloroplasts of plant cells where carbon dioxide is taken in, water and solar energy are absorbed, and food and oxygen are produced according to the formula:

$$6\ CO_2 + 6\ H_2O \rightarrow C_6H_{12}O_6 + 6\ O_2$$

The two ingredients of photosynthesis are carbon-dioxide and water (and light energy). The two products of photosynthesis are sugar and oxygen. What an amazing coincidence that plants and animals are in a delicate equilibrium of life where one species' "waste" products become the food and air for the other species! In fact, what an amazing coincidence that the waste products of the animals (carbon-dioxide and manure) become the food and air (carbon-dioxide) for the plants! These two species—plants and animals—have lived in that delicate equilibrium balancing carbon dioxide, sugar and oxygen (and composted manure) for thousands, perhaps millions of years. How many times have we won the lottery?

The delicate equilibrium of oxygen, carbon dioxide, sugar, and water is even more complex than I have so far described. The process of photosynthesis "fixes" the carbon in the form of sugar, serving as fuel for plants and animals alike. Planet-wide, a majority of the plant forms are grasses and leaves—most of the fixed carbon, the sugar food, is in those grasses and leaves. Humans cannot digest grasses and leaves. How can we get the nourishment that surrounds us? The Intelligent Designer created 150 species of "ruminants", mammals that have multiple stomachs designed to ferment grasses and leaves, to regurgitate the "cud" of fibrous material to enable further chewing and eventual digesting.[286] Sheep and goats, cattle, horses and camels are ruminants that can digest grasses and leaves and produce milk and meat (and clothing) for human consumption. When humans evolved, they began a symbiotic relationship with these animals, first through hunting, later through domesticating and farming. There is a similar food chain in the earth's lakes and streams, seas and oceans—fish can digest seaweed, plankton and algae and humans consume the fish. The process of cultural evolution naturally selected cultures that learned the technology of grain consumption in another form. The tribes that learned to use mortar and pestle to grind mature grass seeds—wheat, oats, rye, barley, corn—to make bread far surpassed the sustainability of the tribes that didn't use this technology. Likewise, the tribes that learned to cook the grains to make them more digestible—especially rice (and beans)—far surpassed the sustainability of the tribes that did not. Cultural evolution naturally selected for survival of these tribes. And the direct consumption of grains (and beans) is more efficient than the indirect consumption of grain nutrients in meat.[287] (More on this below.)

Nitrogen Fixing

There is another amazing "coincidence" in the food chain of proteins. Amino acids are the building blocks of proteins and Nitrogen is the key ingredient of Amino acids (along with carbon, hydrogen and oxygen atoms). Nitrogen is the most plentiful element in Mother Earth's atmosphere, but—here we go again—it is not in a form fit for human consumption. Nitrogen (N2) is a gas that cannot be absorbed in the human lungs—it needs to be chemically converted into Ammonia by the process called "nitrogen fixation".[288] The chemical formula for the Nitrogen fixation cycle is the following:[289]

$$N2 + 8H + 8e \rightarrow 2NH3 + H2$$

As in Carbon fixation, the Nitrogen fixation cycle is performed by plants. However, not all plants can fix nitrogen like they can fix carbon. Only certain kinds of plants—mostly the plants in the category of "legumes"—can perform the Nitrogen Fixation process. Beans, peas, lentils, clovers, alfalfa, and peanuts are some of the most common legumes. These plants perform a life-giving and life sustaining process producing the food we call protein, which is composed of amino acids whose key element is Nitrogen. And another amazing aspect of the Nitrogen fixation cycle is that it is not only found in certain kinds of plants, it is not sufficient to have these plants—the process is completed not by the plants but by "nitrogen-fixing bacteria"—friendly bacteria are the nitrogen fixers—the plants are merely their hosts.[290]

Once the nitrogen is fixed in the legumes by the bacteria, the plants or their fruits—beans, peas, lentils, etc.—become food for animals and humans in the form of proteins. We eat the proteins in the legumes and the digestion process breaks the proteins down into amino acids—or we eat the animals who have eaten the legumes to get our protein. Either way, digestion of the proteins produces the amino acids that are the building blocks of proteins that we need for life sustenance. Our bodies build the proteins we need under the direction of our DNA. These proteins are essential to our survival. So we need to either eat the plants or their fruits, or eat meat to survive. Some humans get most of their protein in the form of plants and their fruits (primarily in third world countries) and some of us get most of our protein in the form of meat (mostly in industrialized 1st world countries). Many of us have meat at every meal. Most nutritionists seem to be telling us that this amount of (red) meat is not good for our health because of "unhealthy saturated fat" embedded in the meat.[291] Some nutritionists claim that the right amount of meat or the leanness of the meat makes a carnivorous diet healthy. Others recommend a vegetarian diet. (Indeed, the vegetarian diet of certain religions seems to be a key factor in their superior life spans.[292]) These healthy diet theories are controversial. But it seems that the theory is clearer regarding the health of our Mother Earth—the vegetarian diet is better for our planet.[293]

Diet for a small planet[294]

Why is a vegetarian diet better for our planet? It is because of the efficiency of the processing of the protein in the vegetarian diet. For example, it takes about 16 pounds of grain to produce one pound of meat in cattle.[295] In other words, humans could be eating 16 pounds of grain or one pound of beef-meat to get the same nutrition. That is a significant difference in the efficiency of the production of protein. Other animals' flesh is somewhat more efficient. It takes 6 pounds of grain to produce one pound of pork in pigs. The best performer is the chicken—3 pounds of grain produce one pound of meat. As the population of Mother Earth continues to grow, efficiency of protein production becomes increasingly important. A vegetarian diet is the best diet for our small planet. Of course, this opinion is based on the assumption of a diet of grain for the animals. Our discussion of "ruminants" above changes the efficiency factor. Ruminants can live on grasses that do not produce edible grains or legumes. Grass-fed cattle, sheep, goats, etc. produce protein without any consumption of grain. Ruminants can provide a very efficient diet of meat. However, the ruminant consumption of grass has a surprising problematic side-effect—the production of methane gas in the digestion process. The passing of gas in grass fed cattle is much worse than in grain-fed cattle.[296] The passing of gas by cattle produces a significant proportion of the "carbon footprint" on planet earth.[297] It seems that both grain-fed and grass-fed meat diets are less friendly to the environment than the vegetarian diet.

But can vegetarians get enough protein in their diet? Yes. If they are careful to diversify their foods and especially if they get a good portion of legumes—beans, peas, and lentils—they will get plenty of protein. But there is one more secret to a nutritious vegetarian diet—in addition to the legumes, they need to also mix in an equal amount of grains—bread, rice, wheat, oats and barley—in order to have all the ingredients for a protein-rich diet. Why? It's all answered in detail in the important book, *Diet for a Small Planet,* by Frances Moore Lappe.[298] Suffice it to summarize her claims as follows. There is protein in every plant and animal. Once the Nitrogen is fixed in the legumes, much of it is preserved either in the flesh of the animals and humans who consume it, or in the "waste products" of the animals and humans (in the manure). Also, it can be passed on through "green manure" as composted legumes. In any case, non-legume plants thrive on the green and brown manure and so the grains and nuts actually contain significant amounts of protein like the legumes do. And as I showed above, the most efficient way to consume protein is in the vegetarian diet rather than the meat diet. However, there are some essential amino acids that are not plentiful enough in vegetation, even in legumes. But as it turns out, the protein in grains and the protein in legumes are very complementary. Grains and seeds tend to have an abundance of certain amino acids (Tryptophan and the Sulfur-Containing amino acids) and legumes tend to have an abundance of other amino acids (Isoleucine and Lysine).[299] Neither legumes nor grains by themselves can produce the quality of protein that meat and eggs have—but both together can. A combination of legumes and grains provides all the necessary amino acids for a protein rich diet. A model for this complementarity of grains and legumes is my winter clothing closet. I can have a huge pile of gloves in the closet so that I have no fear of the cold weather. However, if I go to the closet and find that all the gloves are right-handed, I will end up with a cold left hand in spite of the great number of gloves there. The more balanced the rights and lefts, the more pairs I have and the more people can have both hands warm. It is the same for the grains and legumes—the more balanced the amino acids are, the more usable is the protein. One of the most interesting aspects of this story is how ignorant most of us are about this science and yet how many great cultures have unknowingly practiced this dietary secret for centuries. Think about the classic combinations of beans and rice throughout the world, the Mexican bean and tortilla burrito, the hummus (chick peas) and pita-bread in the Middle East, Couscous and chick peas in North Africa, dal (lentil soup) and rice in India and Bangladesh.[300] These diets contain very little meat but they have been selected for their high-quality protein by means of cultural evolution.[301] The Biblical evidence for this classic combination can be found in Ezekiel 4:9 where the recipe for "Ezekiel Bread" includes "wheat and barley, beans and lentils, millet and spelt"—a survival diet during the Babylonian exile of the Jewish people in the 6th century BC.

But what has diet to do with Intelligent Design theory? Diet is part of the amazing complexity of the science of life and this complexity is much more profound than we have ever known in history. And the complex food chains from "Brother Air" to sugars and amino acids, from Carbon Dioxide to Oxygen, from photosynthesis to nitrogen fixation are more examples of what is called the "Anthropic universe"—it seems like Brother Air has been designed especially for the creation and nutrition of human life. The science of Brother Air points to an Intelligent and Benevolent Designer who has gifted us with Mother Earth. She has been programmed by a Programmer to produce human life and enable it to be nurtured and sustained.

Sister Water

Humans cannot survive without Brother Air for more than a few minutes. We cannot survive without Sister Water for more than a few days. She is the second most important ingredient for human life—for the Anthropic universe. One percent of Brother Air is water in the form of vapor.[302] Seventy-one percent of the surface of Mother earth is water.[303] The oceans contain 97% of the earth's water. Less than 1% of the earth's water is fresh water. "The average human adult male is approximately 60% water and the average adult female is about 55%".[304] Water is one of the key ingredients in photosynthesis, the manufacturing of carbohydrate food for all living things. Sister Water is essential to life and, next to air, the most precious object on Mother Earth. Conservation of water should be our second greatest priority in the ecosystem.

Sister water is peculiar in many ways. She is found in all three phases in our ecosystem—liquid water, frozen ice and water vapor—an unusual phenomenon on planet earth. And one of the most peculiar qualities of water is that it is more dense in its liquid form at 4 degrees Centigrade than in its solid (ice) form.[305] There are a few other elements that have this unusual quality. But with regard to water, the higher density of 4-degree water over ice has critical implications for life. If ice were denser than water, it would not float. It would sink to the bottom of all bodies of water. Water would continue to form ice which would sink until all bodies of water were solid ice before the end of winter in the arctic and temperate zones. Virtually all fish life in these zones would freeze to death. This science could be considered one more example of evidence for the Anthropic Universe—it seems that the Intelligent Designer of Mother Earth designed water to not only sustain human life but also marine life (which is part of the human food chain).

Sister water, like brothers Fire and Wind, can be as unfriendly as it is friendly. As I write this, Hurricanes Harvey and Irma have recently passed through, devastating large parts of Texas and Florida. Sister Water was turned into life-threatening storms by Brothers Wind and Air. Flooding and wind damage destroyed homes and commerce for millions of people. Fortunately, only 50-some lives were lost—it could have been a much larger toll. But why didn't God do something to stop these storms? Jobe Syndrome is often triggered by these kinds of events. We must admit again that we do not know why. However, the science of water and oceans provides part of the answer—massive bodies of water in its liquid form can be heated by the sun to the point that there is a huge increase of warm water vapor rising in the sky and mixing with cold air at higher elevations to produce wind currents that can increase to hurricane levels. This is the nature of water in the oceans. God could alter the natural laws and the science of water, but if this were a frequent phenomenon, then scientists could not develop a science of meteorology and there would be no miracles—hurricanes would always miss landfall for an unknown reason. Science and religion need consistency in natural laws in order to develop science and in order to recognize (occasional) miracles. And what if there were no storms on Mother Earth? Then there would be no rainfall. Without rainfall, there would be no fresh water in our eco-system. Think about it—why do shipwrecked sailors die of thirst in the midst of the ocean? It can be caused by the drinking of seawater.[306] Ninety-seven percent of Mother Earth's water is saltwater—undrinkable. It is the evaporation process of solar heating the seawater that purifies the saltwater to form clouds of pure water vapor free of salt. And it is when the clouds get dense enough with fresh water vapor to condense into rain that storms happen—and Mother Earth is drenched in fresh water, the one percent of the water of the earth that we live on. This is the beautiful side of storms—part of the beautiful picture on the Tapestry of Life. Of course, there is also the backside of the tapestry that we saw in the hurricanes and tornadoes—the backside of the Tapestry of Life. It seems that we can't have the one without the other.

Brother Fire

Brother Fire has the same kind of ambiguity as Brother Wind and Sister Water. It can be Anthropic (human life sustaining) or it can be destructive. Fire has been valued by humans for thousands of years as light in the dark and warmth in the cold. It is valuable for cooking food and indeed it is involved on a micro-scale in every cell of the body (respiration involves the oxidation—the "burning"—of carbon compounds (food) to produce energy). Fire is used in the chemical processing of most elements and compounds produced by modern technology—gold refining, copper and iron production, and countless other products. Brother Fire can be our friend. But like Brothers Wind and Air and Sister Water, Brother Fire can also be destructive. It can destroy homes, forests, businesses, as well as human life. Why doesn't God stop fire from destroying life and property? The same questions emerge as they did with the hurricanes—why? We don't know. This is the view of the backside of the Tapestry of Life. We do know the good aspects of Fire. That's the Design part. That's on the frontside of the Tapestry.

Brother Fire proves the importance of himself in his giant star we call Brother Sun—the sun is the biggest fire in our solar system. Brother Sun is Brother Fire on a grand scale. Without Brother Fire and Brother Sun, Mother Earth would be a frozen planet like Mars. And if the distance between Brother Sun and Mother Earth were much more than 93 million miles, Mother Earth would be a frozen planet. If the distance were much less, the Mother Earth would be a desert planet like Venus. In this line of thinking, we could say that Brother Fire in Brother Sun at 93 million miles distance from us is the most important ingredient to human life—as important as Brother Air and Sister Water. This is part of the front side of the Tapestry of Life—the beautiful picture. This is more evidence that Mother Earth is benevolent—the anthropic principle.

CHAPTER EIGHT

Brother Pain

B rother Pain is not mentioned in St. Francis' hymn of Creation. Perhaps St. Francis did not see any good in pain. That is not surprising. What good can there be in pain? Perhaps pain is the biggest obstacle to belief in an Intelligent Designer who is also a Benevolent Designer. For the atheist or satanist, the feeling of Pain is the evidence that there is no caring God. There is either no God (according to the atheist), or Satan is God ("God is evil", according to the Satanist)—the evidence of pain seems to prove their cases. The atheists say that their position is better than the Satanist view. At least there is no evil God—there is just no God. "It is what it is." This is what is called "The Problem of Evil" or the "Theodicy" [307] or Jobe Syndrome. Why is there evil in a universe created by a loving God? Why is there pain and suffering, especially of the innocent, especially of the children? All we can see is the backside of the Tapestry of Life—the pain and suffering. Can there be any purpose for pain? Can pain contribute anything to the beautiful picture on the frontside of the Tapestry of Life? It seems impossible.

St. Francis did mention "sickness and trial" in his hymn of creation: "Be praised, my Lord...through those who endure sickness and trial. Happy those who endure in peace, for by You, Most High, they will be crowned." St. Francis did claim a reward, a good outcome, for those who endure the pain and suffering of sickness and trial. But he did not call them "Brother sickness" or "Sister trial". It is only in our contemporary world of science that we can find some of the beautiful picture on the front side of the Tapestry. This part of the picture was discovered by Doctor Paul Brand and his discovery was documented in the excellent book, *The Gift of Pain*.[308] Doctor Brand specialized in the study and treatment of Hansen's Disease—Leprosy. He discovered that leprosy was caused by a bacterium that attacked the nervous system—nerve cells. The common thinking for centuries was that leprosy killed the extremities of the body—the fingers, toes, ears and nose, etc. Gradually, these dead parts of the body rotted away. Dr. Brand discovered that the extremities did not rot away because of Hansen's Disease—they rotted away because of injuries to the body parts—infected cuts and bruises and burns and broken bones. And this is the key—the injuries to the body parts occurred because the victims could not feel pain. The bacterium attacks the nerve cells and makes them numb—unable to transmit pain sensation to the brain—so that the victim cannot feel the burning finger or toe, the broken bone, the cut, until so much damage occurred that the extremity often could not be saved. The severe damage to the extremity became infected and gangrene set in. The extremity was lost because the injury did not hurt. Rabbi Harold Kushner found another disease that eliminates pain and causes serious injury—"familial dysautonomia"[309] (FD). FD is a genetic disorder that "affects the development and survival of ... neurons". Symptoms include "less perception in pain or temperature". This can result in "inadvertent self-mutilation". The mutilation of the body is not directly caused by the disorder, but by the lack of pain sensation. This is similar to the case of leprosy. Pain is designed in the body to signal an imminent injury—to protect us from serious injury. When we feel the pain of the hot stove, we pull our hand off the burner immediately, preventing a serious burn (though we may have healable damage). But the victims of Hansen's disease or FD do not feel the burning and do not immediately pull away—their injuries are more serious and often not healable. Can pain be our friend? Can pain really be Brother pain?

Imagine yourself to be the intelligent designer of the first mammal. It is not too different than designing the first car. Each can be considered as an invention of a machine—one made of software and the other made of hardware. Fuel intake is key to both "machines". The mammal has a fuel intake system composed of a mouth and teeth, a fuel digestion system composed of stomach and small and large intestines. Fuel ingestion and digestion are necessary for life. How can you be sure that your animal eats enough food to sustain life? You could put a fuel gauge on the belly of your mammal, but would it work? No. your animal can't read the gauge and even if it could, the animal would not know that there is a connection between "empty" and death. The fuel gauge is useless to your mammal. What else can you do to get the animal to eat? How about linking the need for food to the pain of hunger? When the fuel tank is empty, the animal feels the pain of hunger. In fact, that seems exactly the way the Intelligent Designer designed mammals—hunger keeps the animals on the hunt for food. Hunger keeps the animal eating. But isn't that cruel? Isn't it cruel to use pain to get the animal to eat? The answer is "No"—it is the only way to get the animal to eat. There isn't another way. But why not use pleasure? The pleasure of eating tasty food should work to prevent the animal from starving. But what if there are competing pleasures? What if the animal would rather spend its whole day in sexual activity rather than eating? Sexual orgasm is the most intense pleasure in the body. An irresponsible animal would possibly enjoy sexual activity until it starves. It is the combination of the pleasure of eating and the pain of hunger that keeps the animal vigilant for food throughout the day, preventing starvation. Hunger pain is Brother Pain. Hunger pain is designed to be our friend. However, sometimes there are droughts on planet earth that prevent hunger and thirst to be satisfied and people die in pain—this is part of the backside of the tapestry. That is not what pain was designed for.

But what about other kinds of pain? How can you get your animal to "know" that it is sick and needs to rest? We could again use our example of a car. A car has a temperature gauge—when the needle moves to the red zone, stop the engine! If you don't, then the engine temperature will keep rising until the engine parts warp. Then the engine is broken—it must be replaced. But if the temperature gauge is heeded, the driver shuts down the engine as soon as the needle hits the red zone. The engine is saved. The problem might be solved with the simple addition of some radiator fluid. So why not put a temperature gauge on our animal's tummy? Again, the animal could not read the gauge, and even if it could, it would not know that there is a connection between "hot" and "sick". The animal would keep on operating as it always does. However, if instead of a gauge, our animal "feels" hot and when it does, it experiences aches and pains and drowsiness and it goes to bed. Bedrest is the best thing an animal can do when it is sick. Just like when the bone is broken—the animal must stop moving or compound the injury. Brother Pain gets our attention and gets us to stop moving the injured or ill body—it gets us to rest. Thank God for Brother Pain.

No Pain and No Gain

Athletes know the importance of Brother Pain in their drive to win. I've never seen kids fasting from food and drink like they do on wrestling and boxing teams—starvation diets for 24 hours to get below their weight category—to give them an advantage over the smaller guy that didn't fast. This extreme fasting is not good for one's health so our contemporary athletic associations are improving the regulations and the enforcement of restrictions on fasting. But athletes also practice healthy inflictions of pain on themselves to strengthen their bodies. "Getting in shape" and "working out" and exercise of all kinds and restrictions on unhealthy foods—all these practices tone the muscles, reduce fat and obesity, strengthen the cardio-vascular system and make us stronger and healthier—and they all involve the pain of discipline and exercise. Athletes know when the exercise has begun to tone and strengthen muscles when they wake up the next day with the pain of "stiff" muscles—a sign of an exercised muscle that hasn't been worked out lately. No pain—no gain.

Astronauts learned and taught us an amazing hidden fact—use your muscles or lose them. The prolonged experience of weightlessness—producing no stress on the leg muscles—resulted in the loss of muscle mass and the inability to walk normally for hours after re-entry into earth's gravitation.[310]

Humans need the stress of the force of gravity on our leg muscles in order to maintain muscle mass and the ability to walk. Use those muscles or lose them. Even more problematic is the loss of bone density.[311] So space flights that involve extended periods of weightlessness now include a gymnasium area with daily scheduled workouts for astronauts to prevent muscle and bone atrophy. The pain of exercise is good for our health. Thank God for some stress on our muscles. We only see the backside of the Tapestry—pain and stress. The Intelligent Designer sees the front side of the Tapestry—health and strength and the ability to walk.

The Parable of the Egg

One of the best examples of our need for stress, pain and struggle is the hatching of the baby chicken. Once upon a time there was a mother hen sitting on two eggs. It came time for the eggs to hatch and mister farmer and mother hen were excited to see a tiny hole in each of the eggs—the chicks had started to pick their way through the eggshells. After a few hours, the chicks had made so little headway that mister farmer began to panic. "The chicks will die in their shells if we don't help them out!" And he began to help pick away at one of the shells. "Don't do it!" exclaimed mother hen. "If you crack the shell, baby chick will die. Let baby chick do it herself." Mister farmer responded, "What kind of a mother are you? You are so cruel!" And mister farmer continued to help baby chick out of the shell. Shortly after this, baby chick died but the other baby chick succeeded in pecking herself out of the egg shell—it was alive and healthy. Mister farmer was in terrible grief and confusion. "Why did my chick die and yours live?" Mother hen responded, "I told you not to help baby chick. She needed to struggle her way through that shell in order to build up the muscles she needed to survive. She was too weak even to walk when you pecked her out of it." Mister farmer learned the lesson of the astronauts and the athletes—no pain, no gain—use it or lose it. And what is true of the baby chick is also true of the butterfly. It is dangerous to help a butterfly out of its chrysalis. "In most instances, helping the butterfly out of the chrysalis [which corresponds to the "cocoon" of the moths] will prevent it from ever flying. The butterfly needs the struggle to strengthen its wings".[312] The butterfly teaches us that "the very things we struggle with actually give us the strength and character to become who we are."[313] Thank God for Brother Pain (and stress and struggle).

Palliative Care

Brother Pain is our friend. However, some serious illnesses and injuries produce excessive and unbearable pain. Then pain becomes our enemy. What was designed for our protection sometimes causes us to die in agony. In those cases, the Intelligent Design seems to have lost its Benevolence—it seems like Satan is the designer. No. The Intelligent Designer has designed humans to be intelligent enough to discover anesthetics—chemicals that can numb the pain when it has become excessive and unbearable and no longer useful. These chemicals, like morphine, for example, can be used to comfort the patient when pain is no longer useful. So when we have diagnosed a terminal illness or injury, pain is no longer useful—it has led us to a correct diagnosis. If treatment is possible, treatment should be done. But if treatment is not going to be helpful or successful, or if the treatment is worse than the disease, the patient can choose to finish his or her life with dignity, without treatment and without pain in what is called "palliative care".[314] In palliative care the focus is no longer on treating the disease or injury; it is focused on treating the pain and suffering. Many kinds of drugs are used to control pain and enable the patient to die peacefully. Hospice Centers have experts at palliative care.[315] They have discovered the optimum combinations of drugs and the optimum doses of drugs to make terminally ill patients comfortable. Patients in severe pain can tolerate much higher doses of drugs than persons with less severe pain. Hospice has discovered the usefulness of these much higher doses and they can now control virtually all kinds and all intensities of pain. The sad reality of terminal illness is that too many patients wait until they are on their deathbed before they enter Hospice care—they could have had Hospice assistance for 6 months, but they wait until the very end, missing most of the Hospice support available. Hospice care is so much better than assisted suicide in enabling terminal patients to die with dignity. They can prevent Brother Pain from becoming our enemy.

Redemptive Suffering

Pain can become bearable if it is meaningful. That is one key insight of Victor Frankl in his classic book, *Man's Search for Meaning*.[316] What kind of meaning can suffering have? Both the Buddhists and the Christians teach that pain is everywhere and is inevitable—pain is part of life. The Christians teach something more amazing—that God suffers pain.[317] God suffers with us and God suffers for us—pain and suffering are part of loving and God is Love (1 John 4:8 and 4:16).

The Intelligent Designer-God planned to sacrifice God's Self for Creatures. Why? Why did a God-Who-is-Love include pain and suffering in creation? Why would Love inflict pain? Answer: Original sin. Because of Original Sin there is an epidemic of narcissism. Narcissistic people inflict pain on the ones who love them. Pain is involved with Love. There are at least three words for Love in the Biblical Greek language—*Eros, Philia and Agape. Eros* is the passionate love between lovers—the drive toward sexual union. This is the Love that is celebrated in the Bible book, the "Song of Songs". Then there is *Philia*— the love of friendship—the non-sexual love between two people that care about each other, who really enjoy being together, doing everything together, sharing interests. This is the love of friendship that Peter had for Jesus (John 21:15-17). But Jesus taught that these loves are not enough (Luke 6:32). Jesus taught and lived *Agape* love—love that sacrifices self for others:

> "For God so loved the world, that He gave His only begotten Son, that whoever believes in Him shall not perish, but have eternal life." (John 3:16).

> "For the Son of Man did not come to be served but to serve and to give his life as a ransom for many." (Mark 10:45)

Why did Jesus have to die from torture? Why did God have to sacrifice his own Son? Because of sin. If the original sin had never been committed, there would be no need for *Agape* Love—for sacrifice. But as soon as the first selfish act occurred, everybody suffered from it and selfishness became epidemic.

As soon as selfishness became epidemic, then everybody experienced being a victim of suffering and everyone felt the need for self-defense—the need to construct walls for the protection of self—and the need for revenge. Everyone sinned and became addicted to selfishness. Everyone suffers from Narcissism. We have seen above that this condition of selfishness functioned in evolution as a necessary aspect of natural selection. But once human beings evolved, then natural selection became sin. This dynamic will be explained in more detail in Chapter 10 on the Second Death. It is enough for this discussion to know that it would take a monumental act of sacrifice of self to overcome the epidemic of selfishness on planet earth—it would take an infinite sacrifice of Self. That is the Christian belief in the sacrifice of Jesus on the cross—the infinite sacrifice that is re-enacted in every celebration of the Lord's Supper every day throughout the world. Christians believe that the self-sacrifice of Jesus on the cross liberated people from the bondage of selfishness. Selfishness no longer rules the world— *Agape* rules the world. God is *Agape* (1 John 4:8 and 16). God is unselfish. God is Altruistic. And Love requires unselfishness. In other words, Love hurts. True Love involves some pain and suffering.

Many Christians leave our discussion at this point. Many Christians believe that Jesus' sacrifice, altruism and *Agape* love fixed the world once and for all. But some Christians remember Jesus' exhortation to "take up your cross and follow me" (Luke 9:23). All of the disciples need not only to experience *Agape* but also to practice *Agape*. All disciples must take up the cross, deny themselves and follow Jesus. St. Paul says it most radically:

> "Now I rejoice in my sufferings for your sake,
> and in my flesh I am filling up what is lacking
> in the afflictions of Christ on behalf of his body,
> which is the church…" (Colossians 1:24)

This is an amazing claim by St. Paul. What could be lacking in the Sacrifice of Christ? Apparently, what is lacking in the sufferings of Christ is our own decision to participate in his sacrifice—our own decision to "take up [our] cross and follow" Jesus. Christians are called by Christ to do this—to give *Agape* once we have received *Agape*. When Christians spread *Agape* Love—altruism—unselfishness—around, they enable others to experience the effects of the sacrifice of Jesus in their own generation—to experience God who is unselfish. This "fills up what is lacking" in Jesus' sacrifice and it extinguishes the epidemic of narcissism. Christians are called by Christ to follow him in his passion. Not everyone believes this, let alone practices it. When we do suffer pain, we can offer it up to God as a sacrifice—a "spiritual sacrifice" in the words of St. Peter:

> "And like living stones, let yourselves be built
> into a spiritual house to be a holy priesthood
> to offer spiritual sacrifices acceptable to God
> through Jesus Christ." (1 Peter 2:5)

> "But you are a chosen race, a royal priesthood…"
> (1 Peter 2:9)

The Bible book of Revelation calls Christians "priests" in two verses (1:6 and 5:10).

Christians are members of the lay priesthood who offer their "spiritual" sacrifices along with the sacrifice of Jesus.

> All their works, prayers, and apostolic endeavors, their ordinary married and family life, the hardships of life, if patiently borne, become "spiritual sacrifices acceptable to God through Jesus Christ" (1 Peter 2:5). In the celebration of the Eucharist, these [spiritual sacrifices] may most fittingly be offered along with the body of the Lord.[318]

The action of the liturgy of the Eucharist incorporates these "spiritual sacrifices" of Christians into the Sacrifice of Christ, an infinite sacrifice. The real-life sacrifices made present in this sacrament have the power to redeem the world. Redemptive suffering and pain makes pain worth suffering. Brother pain can change the world if he is offered up to God for others. And Christians have the wonderful assurance that our God suffers along with us.[319] And Christians believe that God's suffering in the person of Jesus liberated the world from selfishness, sin and death.

CHAPTER NINE

Sister Death

The bottom line in our discussion of the Tapestry of Life is death—if everything ends in death, then isn't that evil? Isn't the Intelligent Designer sadistic? Where is the benevolence? Wait a minute! Is life worthless if it only lasts 70 or 80 or 90 years? Would you prefer never to have been born rather than to have 80 or 70 or even 20 years of life? I would love to have my 70 or 80 years whether or not it ends in death. Every moment of life is a gift from the Intelligent Designer. Thank God for life—and thank God for Sister Death.

Imagine what Mother Earth would be like if there were no death—if everyone were immortal and lived forever. Think of how many people would be barely surviving on planet earth. At this writing we have about 8 billion people on earth. Mother Earth has thus far proven to be able to sustain this population. We do not know how many people have ever lived on our planet. However, if we begin with the Roman Empire alone, estimates range from around 50 to 90 million people. This has been estimated to be 20 % of the world's population in the beginning of the 1st millennium.[320] That means that the population of the whole world at the beginning of the first millennium A.D. was about 250 million to 450 million people. Let's use the lower estimate—1/4 billion people. If a generation is about 30 years, and if every couple produced 2 children every 30 years, then the population of planet earth would have doubled every 30 years—every generation. (This is what is called a geometric progression.) That would mean that by 30 AD, there would have been ½ billion people; by 60 AD, 1 billion; by 90 AD, 2 billion; by 120 AD, 4 billion; by 150 AD, 8 billion; by 180 AD, 16 billion people—twice the current population of planet earth. By the year 210 AD, Mother Earth would have had 32 billion people—even by today's standards we cannot feed 32 billion people (more than four times our current population). The human race would have starved to death by the end of the second century. If we calculated today's population, the 60 plus generations of reproduction on planet earth would have produced a population of more than 4 trillion people! By the mercy of the Intelligent Designer, Sister Death limits us to 70, 80 or 90 years on this planet. Thank God for Sister Death.

But what if Sister Death is not death at all? What if she is actually a form of Birth? What if, at the moment of Death, the bio-field of the human person leaves the human body and is transported into a new dimension of life—a new universe? The bio-field—the soul—separates from the body like the baby separates from the mother. The bio-field—the soul— enters into a new invisible reality, not made up of atoms, but of energy—intelligent energy—just as real as the atoms from which it is "born". This changes everything. It reminds me of the parable of the Triplets.

The Parable of the Triplets[321]

The womb is a wonderful place to be—constant warm temperature, constant satisfaction of food and drink, automatic elimination of waste, always very comfortable floating in water. Who would ever want to leave that world? This is the story of the triplets. Once upon a time there were identical triplets in the mother's womb. These triplets were very superior in their intelligence to any previous or future fetuses. They could communicate with each other by the time they were in their third trimester. It was about this time that the one named "Naïve" said,

"Boy, is it getting crowded in here!"

"Skeptic" responded,

"Get used to it. We are all growing and the womb is getting tighter. The end is near."

Naïve: "What do you mean, the end is near?"

Skeptic: "Isn't it obvious? There is no room for us to grow. We are going to starve and suffocate in a few weeks. We will soon die."

Naïve: "Is that true, Faith?"

(Faith is the third triplet.) "No, Naïve, it is not true."

Naïve: "Then what is going to happen to us?"

Faith: "In a few weeks, we are going to squeeze through that hole and enter a whole new world."

Naïve: "Squeeze through that hole? That is going to hurt!"

Faith: "It will hurt for a short time. But soon after the pain, we are going to see our Mother for the first time and She will take care of us. It's a better world than we have ever known."

Naïve: "WOW!

Skeptic: "Don't believe her! It's a lie—or it's a delusion. There is no other world. There is no Mother. There is only death, the end of life.

Naïve: "Oh no! Faith, how do you know there is another world? A better world? A Mother out there?"

Faith: "I know there is a better world out there because we have a Mother and she will take care of us. I know we have a Mother because I can feel her heartbeat. It is her body that surrounds us and nourishes us and keeps us warm. It is She who created us."

Skeptic: "Nonsense. Show me the Mother."

Faith: "She surrounds us with her body and nurtures us with these cords. We will all see her when we go through that hole."

Naïve: "Who can I believe?"

Faith: "Just ask yourself where we came from? How did we get here? What is that heartbeat? We came from Someone whose heartbeat we feel and whom we shall meet on the other side of that hole—soon."

Skeptic: "There is no heartbeat—it's just your imagination. You are only feeling your own heartbeat."

Suddenly there was an earthquake and all the water disappeared through the hole. A series of earthquakes followed that shook and squeezed the womb over and over.

Naïve screamed and struggled away from the hole. Skeptic also climbed away from the hole.

Faith crawled toward the hole. "Don't be afraid", she said. "We are being born into a whole new world." And Faith disappeared through the hole.

"This is the end," said Skeptic.

"I wonder," said Naïve.

And at least two of them lived happily ever after.

If Sister Death is not a death at all—if she is only a new kind of birth from the womb of Mother Earth into a whole new dimension of space and time in another universe—then what is so bad about Sister Death—why do people call it evil? First, it seems evil if you don't believe that there is life after death. It seems like death is the end of life. But if death is really a birth, then death is not evil. It can be painful—like childbirth—but the pain is transitory and it ends in a new and better dimension of life, a new universe. Sister Death is not evil. Secondly, death feels evil because it separates us from beloved people in our life. The pain of separation is real, but it also is temporary—all our loved ones, sooner or later, will join us in birth into the new and better world outside the womb of Mother Earth. Sister death is painful, but temporarily so—she is not evil. But how can someone continue to exist without their body?

The Human Bio-field is Immortal

We have proposed above (in chapter five) the existence of the bio-field. The bio-field is the force field that pulls bio-chemicals into spheres that respire, ingest fuel, eliminate waste, reproduce. The bio-field exerts the force of life. Its most basic unit is the cell-field that organizes the cell. It becomes more complex and stronger as it combines cells into plants and animals in the process of evolution. The Cambrian explosion[322] greatly increased the complexity of the bio-fields, producing the current peak of the evolution process—the human being. The bio-field of the human being is the most complex and intelligent—the human brain is more advanced than any computer—it invented the computer. It is so much more advanced that it needs to be honored in a whole different category than the brains of primates. The human bio-field has been called the "soul". In metaphysics, the soul is immortal—once it comes into existence it continues forever (e.g., John 6:50-51). How can this be? The soul is created at the moment of conception when sperm and egg unite. The soul's intelligence and willpower develop along with the human body. When the human body dies, all signs of life disappear. How could the soul continue after the body dies? Can the soul survive without a body?

The human soul is the most complex bio-field in the world. Once the human bio-field is created, it continues to develop its complexity, its knowledge and memory storage long after the body achieves its peak physical development (approximately 20 years old?). Even while the body is declining in physical strength and health, the human bio-field continues to develop in complexity, knowledge, memory and will. And the human bio-field is not restricted to its location in the brain of the human body. This is the key. And this key was only recently discovered along with the great advance in technology in the 20 the century. With the invention of the telegraph came the experience of communication the length of the continent (or the length of the transmission lines). With the invention of the telephone came the transmission of voices the length of the continent (or the length of the transmission lines). With the invention of the radio came the experience of voices without transmission lines—wireless transmission of voices. With the invention of the TV came the wireless transmission of video as well as sound. With the launching of the communications satellites came the transmission of video and sound to anywhere on Planet Earth—with a "quarter of a second"[323] delay. Today, we can see and hear each other instantaneously by using SKYPE[324] or FACETIME[325] or other communication technology in the "noosphere"[326]—the internet—and it's just like being there in our family's living room across the continent or around the world. The only missing senses are touch and smell and taste—sight and sound are available everywhere. So where am I when I am "Skyping" my family? Am I in my living room or theirs? My sound and my image are in both places, are they not? Not only are my image and my voice in both living rooms—Michigan and North Carolina—but they are also everywhere in between. My electromagnetic signal travels through space at the speed of light, bounces off the communications satellite in space and rebounds to earth in my family's living room—my image and sound are everywhere along that line. In fact, I could SKYPE the international space station and see and hear the astronauts. If we had another moon landing, I could SKYPE the astronauts on the moon! When the astronauts landed on the moon, we were there seeing what they were seeing and hearing their voices. In fact, the signals from my living room continue at the speed of light through outer space and if there are intelligent aliens on some planet in the universe visible to planet earth, my signal will land there and they could see and hear me, if they have invented the technology. The electromagnetic waves continue through space forever if they miss all the stars and planets in their direction.

The human bio-field has the same qualities as the SKYPE technology. The bio-field, once created, complexified and developed, continues to vibrate its life-waves even after the body dies. It sees and hears and tastes, smells and touches anywhere in space-time. It can penetrate walls, see what was invisible to the eye. The human bio-field has the same qualities as electromagnetic fields and waves and more. The human bio-field is invisible, able to travel through space-time at the speed of light. Above all, the human bio-field is conscious and aware after death—it is the human soul. Once the soul makes the transition from our universe to the other—once it is "born again" (John 3) into the next life, it can see the other side of the Tapestry of Life. The soul can meet GOD—seeing the Beatific Vision[327], "the ultimate direct self-communication of God", feeling the infinite benevolence of GOD, and hearing heavenly sounds. The human soul can experience ecstasy. But is there any evidence for the soul leaving the dead body behind?

Near Death Experiences (NDEs)

The most recent evidence for the soul leaving the body comes from a large number of testimonies of people who have experienced death and have been resuscitated. This body of evidence is especially large in recent literature because of our significant advances in medical technology in the 20th century and beyond. We are now routinely re-starting the heartbeat of patients in hospitals after cardiac arrest. Emergency Medical Technicians (EMTs) routinely resuscitate victims of heart attacks and auto accidents. So many more people than ever before in history have experienced death and have come back to life. Near death experiences (NDEs) are commonplace in the medical world like never before. NDE is a misnomer in the cases I am highlighting. These cases involve patients who have not only come close to death, but rather have actually died according to a medical definition of death. Death can be defined as the stopping of heart activity and/or the stopping of brain activity. Many of those who have testified to their consciousness after death have medical evidence of their heart stoppage or brain waves "flatlining". Dr. Raymond Moody has spent much of his medical career studying the testimonies of people whose hearts have stopped and who report their experiences during the heart stoppage. In his book, *Life after Life*[328], Moody documented the cases of several patients who could describe what they saw and heard while their bodies were dead. He also documented a few cases in which he was "able to get the independent testimony of others about corroborating events".[329] Many patients reported similar experiences of the Light, the tunnel, the meeting of other beings and of deceased relatives.[330] Dr. Melvin Morse documented many cases of children giving their testimonies of what they experienced during their NDEs in his book, *Closer to the Light*.[331] Many people find the testimonies of children even more believable than the adult testimonies. The children's testimonies were very similar to the adult cases in Moody's Book. The recent movie "Breakthrough" documents the true story of a 10-year-old boy who was dead for 45 minutes (and fully recovered).[332]Doctor Eben Alexander provided a neurosurgeon's perspective on his near-death experience in his book, *Proof of Heaven*.[333] NDEs have produced a whole new genre of literature documenting so many testimonies of people experiencing conscious life outside their bodies.[334]

The Resurrection of Jesus

The most famous evidence for life after death comes from the Christian faith—the central teaching of the Christian gospel is that Jesus of Nazareth rose from the dead on the third day. The soul of Jesus animated a new glorified body after two days in the tomb. The faith also teaches that during his two days in the tomb, Jesus' soul left his body and "descended to the dead" where he preached the gospel of life to people who had died. (1 Peter 3:18-20 and 4:6) After he rose from the dead, he appeared to his disciples during the next 40 days. (Acts 1:3). St. Paul claims to have seen Jesus long after the 40 days (1 Cor. 15:8) and he claims that at one point, 500 disciples saw Jesus at the same event (1 Cor. 15:6). The women disciples were the first to find and testify to the empty tomb, followed by the 11 apostles and many other disciples. The testimony of the empty tomb became public knowledge on or before the Pentecost event, 50 days after the Easter resurrection (Acts 2). The credibility of the testimony of the empty tomb rests on at least two key factors—the number of witnesses and the quality of their testimony. First, the publicity of the events enabled there to be hundreds of witnesses to the empty tomb. If the testimony had been fabricated, the Roman government, the Jewish government or any interested individual could have checked out the story by locating the tomb themselves and finding the dead body. There is no evidence of this happening. There is some evidence that the Jewish authorities claimed that the disciples of Jesus stole and hid the body. (Matthew 28:11-15) This claim ironically confirms the testimony of the disciples that Jesus' tomb was empty—no one could produce the body. So the testimony of the empty tomb is apparently confirmed by both the disciples and the enemies of Jesus. All that remains is the question of whether or not Jesus' body was stolen and hidden. That is the question of the quality of the witnesses. The 120 disciples who experienced the Pentecost event (Acts 1:15) became the primary witnesses to the empty tomb. We don't know how all these witnesses ended their lives, but we do have traditions on virtually all of the 12 apostles—Jesus' inner circle—that claim that 11 of them were tortured to death. John alone died a natural death (John 21:18-23). The quality of these witnesses is related to the concept of the "Dying declaration"[335]. The dying declaration "constituted the last words of a dying person. The rationale…is that someone who is dying or believes death to be imminent would have less incentive to fabricate testimony". All of the disciples took their testimony to their graves—no one recanted on their deathbed. This adds credibility to the testimonies of the disciples. But the disciples not only gave their dying declarations for the record—they withstood torture in their dying. Peter was crucified upside down on a cross; James was beheaded; Andrew was crucified on an X-shaped cross; Bartholomew was skinned alive and crucified[336]. All of their deaths came from torture. The executioners invited all of them to retract their testimony in exchange for acquittal—all they had to do was to deny the Jesus story and they would have been released. But they didn't. Holding on to their testimony under penalty of torture is a significant step higher than the Dying declaration—which is a significant step above ordinary testimony.[337] The quality as well as the quantity of testimonies to Jesus' life after death is amazing. Jesus continues to provide the best evidence for life after death in the history of the world. Lee Strobel documents the journalistic evidence in The Case for Christ.[338] So Jesus' followers actually believe in three births—birth from the womb, the "born-again" second birth from the Baptism water to the family of God (John 3:3-7), and the third birth from human life through Sister Death into the eternal life in ecstatic union with God. Sister Death is actually Sister Birth into the Heavenly City of God (Revelation 21:22-27).

One final testimony of the Jewish Roman Historian, Josephus:

> Now there was about this time, Jesus, a wise man, if it be lawful to call him a man, for he was a doer of wonderful works—a teacher of such men as receive the truth with pleasure. He drew over to him both many of the Jews and many of the Gentiles. He was [the] Christ;

and when Pilate, at the suggestion of the principal men among us, had condemned him to the cross, those that loved him at the first did not forsake him, for he appeared to them alive again the third day, as the divine prophets had foretold…and the tribe of Christians, so named from him, are not extinct at this day.[339]

CHAPTER 10

Mortal Sin and the Second Death

In his Hymn to Creation, St. Francis emphasized the beauty of all Creation and the Benevolence he saw in every aspect of it, including Sister Death. In doing so, he was giving us a glimpse of the beautiful side of the Tapestry of Life, the side seen by the Intelligent Designer and all the souls who have transitioned through physical death, the third birth, after having been "born again" (John 3:3-7). But he did mention two very negative realities, two great evils—"mortal sin" and the "second death". Because they are evil, they are not Brother or Sister or Mother or Father. And they are not creatures of the Intelligent and Benevolent Designer-God. The Designer only designs good creatures: "God looked at everything he had made, and found it very good" (Genesis 1:31). Nothing designed by the Benevolent Designer is evil. But where did these great evils come from? Human beings and Alien beings. Everything that is evil has come from human sin and the sin of the "fallen" angels. Some sins are "venial" and others are "mortal" or "deadly" (1 John 5:16-17). Mortal sin leads to the "second death"—death of the soul. This is a state of permanent narcissism—where the soul is addicted to selfishness and self-worship. There is selfishness and there is addiction to selfishness—narcissism. This is the state of a soul who worships itself, who makes oneself god. Narcissism is the root of all idolatry—all kinds of creature-worship. Addiction to money, addiction to pleasure and addiction to power and fame—all these are forms of narcissism and self-worship and idolatry. All these lead to mortal sin and the "second death".

Narcissism, Hedonism[340] and selfishness are as old as human beings, but modern psychology and philosophy have brought forth new versions of these lifestyles. Freudian psychology and Ayn Rand "Objectivism",[341] for example, relabel selfishness as neither good nor evil or even as "good". Ayn Rand referred to egoism as "the virtue of selfishness".[342] It is interesting that both of these 20th century thinkers are anti-religion and anti-God. And this kind of thinking influenced movements like the Hippies, the sex revolution and the drug revolution. "Do what feels good" is the Hippie version of the ancient Hedonism.[343] Without an Intelligent Designer as the source of the design of natural law, there is no foundation for ethics other than the self. If there is no Supreme Intelligent Designer, there is no one left to worship than one's self. What about family and friends? Don't many of us sacrifice ourselves for family and friends? Aren't we in some sense worshipping our family and friends? Yes. Family and friends can be the objects of "worship" for an atheist or agnostic. But there is always a significant return they get from their family and friends—there is a payback to myself that is not truly altruistic or unselfish. Altruism is the sacrificing of one's self for other(s) who will not or cannot pay me back. (Matt 5:46-48) Altruism is not possible without the presence of a Supreme Intelligent Designer who designs natural law with an incentive to be unselfish and altruistic. But what is an incentive to be altruistic? Isn't incentive and altruism an oxy-moron? Altruism negates incentive?

We have seen above (in chapter 3) the attempt of socio-biologists to explain altruism in human beings. They use the ant-hill or the beehive to demonstrate the survival advantage of insects who organize and cooperate in an ant or bee culture that is so much stronger than the sum of its individual members. This organization includes slave labor of the worker bees. It also includes defense against enemies of the hive where soldier bees fight and die to protect the hive. Some bees "volunteer" on the front lines of attack. Why do they do it? Socio-biologists say that it is caused by the presence of the "selfish gene" in each individual—the worker ant or soldier bee has genetics in common because all ants and all bees are offspring of the same mother—the Queen Bee or Queen Ant—all the individuals in the hive are related as half brothers and sisters. Ants and bees sacrifice themselves to preserve their own selfish genes.

But that is not the case in human culture—the vast majority of individuals in the culture do not have genetics in common (except for remote ancestors). Humans naturally and instinctively behave altruistically toward their own close family members because of genetics—Family members share many of the same genes. But this does not explain the sacrifice of life and wealth and power and possessions that is intrinsic to society on a national scale. All nations are dependent upon the taxes, armies, labor of their citizens—the cooperation with the laws of the state in general—to function as a nation. The strongest nations—most suited for survival—are those whose members cooperate in a very complex structure. All other things being equal, the nations most suited for survival are those whose members cooperate like bees in the beehive—and that includes many members who are willing to sacrifice their lives to defend the nation. That is a level of altruism a step above that of family members with common genetics. But does the soldier benefit from this altruism? Yes. Having a strong nation makes it a safer place to live than in a weak nation. The soldier's chances of survival are much better in a strong and cooperative army or nation than in a weak and uncooperative one. And safer also for one's family to live. Does this payback negate the altruism of the soldier? No. It is still altruistic because I offer my life as a soldier and may lose it for the sake of the nation. I may not benefit as an individual from my sacrifice. This qualifies as altruism. But it is not yet the level of altruism in cultures where there is a common belief in an Intelligent and Benevolent Designer—God.

The belief in an Intelligent and Benevolent Designer enables us to take altruism to the next level. The soldier in a strong nation will risk his life to protect the nation (including her family), but the devoted believer in the Intelligent and Benevolent Designer is sometimes motivated to sacrifice her life because the Designer "tells her" to do so out of love for a person who is not a citizen of my nation nor a member of my family. So we have mentioned above (in chapter 6) the likes of Maximillian Kolbe, Catherine of Siena, Mother Teresa of Calcutta, Father Damian the leper and many other saints who have taken altruism to the highest level of self-sacrifice—offering to be executed for another prisoner, nursing people during the Black Plague, housing and nursing the homeless dying beggars on the sidewalks of Calcutta, living and ministering among lepers, giving up marriage and family, giving up paychecks for their labor (all checks for Religious order members are made out to the order, not to the individual), etc. How does the Designer "tell them" to do something (or not to do) something? There is the "voice" of the Designer in the conscience of the believer—the "voice" of conscience is a communication device of the Intelligent Designer-God. That "voice"—moral thoughts occurring in one's mind—is what leads some believers to great heights of altruism. And as a result, many have sacrificed their lives for "the poor"—people who are the weakest members of society. The believers in eugenics[344] (e.g., Adolf Hitler and Margaret Sanger[345]) claimed that it was good for society to reduce or eliminate reproduction of the weakest members of society. The saints who followed Jesus believed that the weakest members of society have a special place in the heart of God and deserved special favors of protection and sustenance. The prediction of Christian believers is that a society based on the "preferential option for the poor"[346] is the society best suited for natural selection and survival, contrary to the philosophy of Eugenics. All self-centered societies will end in destruction. The society based on *Agape* (unselfish Love—1 Corinthians 13) will last forever—it is the only society that is sustainable.

But what is the motivation of the altruists? First, there is the law of the Intelligent Designer who is the Supreme Force in the universe. The Intelligent Designer has created law and order in the universe and part of that order includes a law of cooperation, specialization and a degree of mutual self-sacrifice for the common good of society—the motivation of the altruist is to be in the good graces of the Designer-God. Loyalty to the Designer and human society demands some self-sacrifice and that pays off in sustainability—the society that cooperates (like the beehive) is more fit for natural selection and survival than is a hedonistic and disorganized society. I and my family want to be part of a society that is sustainable.

But that only explains level one altruism. Level two altruism of the "saints" goes beyond the motivation of the good citizen. The saints give up family and even their own lives for the Designer and for other fellow human beings. What is their motivation? First of all, the motivation of fear is not present in the saints—"perfect love casts out fear" (1 John 4:18-21). The saints have experienced that the Intelligent Designer is also Benevolent—the universe is life-giving, caring and nurturing. The saints need not fear for their well-being—they trust in the protection of the Benevolent Designer of the universe. The universe is loving and lovable. (The saints see a glimpse of the front side of the Tapestry of Life). But what about death? What do the saints get from dying for others? Remember, death is Sister Death—she is not death but birth. The saints get their reward by passing through Sister Death into the ecstasy of the Beatific Vision of the Intelligent and Benevolent Designer-God—and they get to see the whole front side of the Tapestry of Life in all its glory.

Original Sin

Part of the strategy of hedonists is to deny the reality of "sin" and to declare that there is no such thing as good and evil—or to declare selfishness and narcissism as "good". One perceptive modern psychiatrist, Karl Menninger, asked "Whatever Became of Sin?[347] Our contemporary culture has eliminated the concept of sin and demonized the concept of guilt. We have noted above how the "conscience" is used by the Intelligent Designer of Natural Law to communicate with the human mind and will—the conscience is "God's voice". God communicates to the human body the assembly manual of life by means of the DNA language—God communicates to the human soul the Natural Moral Law by means of "conscience". The strong feelings of "guilt" and "goodness" in the conscience are built into the human soul by the Intelligent Designer to encourage her to do the good and avoid evil. The feelings of goodness empower us to be unselfish—the feelings of guilt punish us for selfishness. Both feelings are "good" because they point us to the good and give us "knowledge of good and evil" (Genesis 2:17). The tree of the knowledge of good and evil in the garden of Eden was good—it empowered Adam and Eve with free will. Free will is good—without free will, humans cannot be good or evil—they could not love or sin. So free will is good—choosing selfishness is evil—sin. But why would God, the Intelligent Designer, create creatures that can sin? That can reject God? Hurt others? Because the Intelligent Designer is also Benevolent—unselfish. God is Love (1 John 4:8 and 16) and Love is unselfish (*agape* love) and Love wants to share Love. And we can't have Love without freedom—free will—Love and freedom go together—Love and coercion are opposed to each other. And so, God chose to give up God's control over human decisions.

Imagine an ignorant and selfish human being who wants a particular beautiful woman. He is unsure of himself, so he gets a gun and points it to her head and says, "You will now be my girlfriend. You will be with me whenever I want you to; you will have sex with me whenever I want you to. You will give me presents on Christmas, on my birthday, and on our anniversary. You will turn all your paychecks over to me. You will love me as long as I want you." Will this woman love such a human being? No. A gun and "Love" are mutually exclusive. Similarly, if God "zapped" humans with a lightning bolt whenever we sinned, everyone would indeed stop sinning out of the fear of God. But they would not experience Love. Love and freedom always go together. So Love (God) could have had a universe of robots who acted like God programmed them to—or Love could have created beings who had free will and were capable of loving—of experiencing Love. That was God's plan. So God created the wonderful tree of the knowledge of good and evil and with that tree came the potential to choose evil (Genesis 3:2-5). Adam and Eve were the first humans capable of loving—and capable of sinning. Sure enough—they chose to sin. The Original Sin.

The vision of Theistic Evolution of Fr. Teilhard de Chardin was criticized and censured by the Church perhaps primarily because he appeared to ignore the doctrine of original sin[348]. But sin defined as selfishness is clearly a prominent theme in evolution theory. Selfishness was present in animals—indeed in all life—before humans became conscious of it. In fact, the selfishness intrinsic in the process of evolution is strong evidence for the reality of original sin—selfishness is ubiquitous and a constant pressure on our behavior. As soon as the first humans evolved, the first humans chose to sin the Original Sin. In some sense, the Intelligent Designer knew that the Original Sin was inevitable—humans were going to choose selfishness rather than love. In fact, we have seen above how selfishness was built into the evolution process—natural selection causes the survival of the fittest species—the selfish plants and animals evolve in a food chain that favors the stronger to defeat the weaker mutations and the Selfish Gene[349] does battle to the death of the weaker genes in order to survive. Selfishness is key to the evolution process—human beings would not have evolved without it. However, as soon as the first primates became sufficiently intelligent to become self-aware of selfishness vs. Love—as soon as "conscience" evolved in the human soul—instantly, humans became humans and they became aware of the "Tree of Knowledge of Good and Evil". And as soon as the first humans became aware of their power to choose selfishness or Love, they repressed the voice of conscience and chose selfishness. And as soon as they chose selfishness they experienced guilt—a warning from the Designer-God that they had made a bad choice—an evil choice—and sin entered Mother Earth. Guilt is to the human soul what pain is to the human body—a warning sign of imminent serious injury. And rather than responding to the guilt feelings with better choices, humans kept responding to the original sin with revenge and an epidemic of sin ensued. And the more that sin pervaded human cultures, the more the voice of conscience and guilt became numbed by the repetition of sin. The voice of Love was repressed. Sin became an addiction and abuse. God could not stop free-willed human beings from choosing self-ishness—and human beings would not stop sinning. They became addicts to the self—narcissists and "idolaters". They worshipped the Self rather than God/Love.

The original sin was a "deadly" sin, often called "mortal sin"—sin so serious that it can lead to the "second death", the death of the soul. There is mortal sin and there is "venial" sin, selfishness that is less than narcissism. (1 John 5:16-17) We can be cleansed of venial sin and selfishness by reparation, prayer, almsgiving (giving to others) and fasting (denying self) in this life and /or in the next life (in the state of "purgatory"). But "there is sin that is mortal" (1 John 5:16). Mortal sin is selfishness to the extreme of narcissism and addiction to self-worship. This condition leads to the "second death", the death of the soul. Like the third birth (from human existence through "death" into the eternal life in ecstatic union with God), the second death is not really death at all—the human soul remains conscious and aware outside of the body. The second death is a "birth process" where consciousness leaves the body behind. But rather than birth into the ecstatic union with the Supreme Designer of the universe, the second death is birth into the solitary state of worshipping oneself by oneself. (No one else will worship me.) The second death produces extreme loneliness and the terrible pain of shame that I am unlovable. This is the state of being addicted to narcissism—I can't / won't let go of my need to be god—to be worshipped. I am stuck in "hell". God keeps trying to change the direction of the person heading toward hell—God never gives up trying. (God does not believe in the death penalty.) God (in Jesus) actually "descended into hell"[350] to "proclaim the gospel even to the dead" (1 Peter 4:6 and 3:19-20). But the addicted narcissist actually locks his own gate to prevent anyone who will not worship him to enter (so no one enters). Hell is the eternal isolation of self—eternal loneliness—the "second death."

The Parable of the Two Banquets

One of the best parables I have heard about hell is the story of the Heavenly Banquet. This is the story of the judgment where the recently deceased man named John met St. Peter at the gate.

"Welcome home," Peter said. "Come and enter the Kingdom prepared for you from all eternity."

"Does that mean I'm going to heaven?"

"You sure are! Your name is written in the Book of Life. You will have eternal bliss with God at the Heavenly banquet."

"Yeay!! Thanks be to God!"

Then he asked Peter, "Before I go to the Heavenly banquet, can I get just one glimpse of hell?"

"Sure you can. Right this way."

Then Peter opened the door to hell and they looked inside. The scene was unbelievable. There was a gigantic banquet room with glorious chandeliers, linen, lace and glass, and centerpieces the likes of which could only be compared to the Grand Hotel Ballroom. And in the center was the largest and most glorious buffet filled with every kind of gourmet dish, fruits, vegetables, wines and desserts—every kind of food imaginable. But all the people in hell were suffering, emaciated and starving to death.

"St. Peter, why are all these people emaciated and starving to death surrounding this amazing banquet? Why don't they just eat to their hearts' content?"

"No one will feed them."

"But why don't they just feed themselves?

"Because they have no elbows. They can't move the food from the plate to the mouth."

"Wow! That is so sad!"

After a few more minutes of meditation on the amazing spectacle, John had had enough of hell.

"Can I go to heaven now?"

"Of course, you can. Follow me." And he did.

St. Peter opened another giant door and there it was, the heavenly banquet!

"Why this looks just like hell," John remarked with unbelief. Except here the people are laughing and talking and eating and drinking to the hearts' content! Oh, I get it—these people have elbows!"

"No," St. Peter responded. "These people also do not have elbows."

"Then how is it that they are so happy and satisfied?"

St. Peter explained: "They feed each other."

John learned a great lesson that day. The people in hell are tortured by their own selfishness, narcissism and self-worship. They cannot stand to be in the presence of God Who is infinite Love (Agape Love, self-sacrificing Love). Yet they do not allow God to cleanse them of their selfishness (by "purgation"). They hold on to the very source of the problem—their narcissism—rather than "Let it Go and Let God in". The people in hell are like the monkey who starved to death because he would not let go of the banana in the glass jar and his clenched hand would not let him fit through the narrow opening of the jar. All he needed to do was to let go of that banana, pull out his empty hand and proceed to pour the banana out to his bowl—the people in hell will not let go of the Self, even though it is killing them.

Jesus of Nazareth

We have seen above (in chapter 6) that without devotion to the Intelligent and Benevolent Designer-God, human beings are stuck with worshipping idols—they are stuck in their addiction to self-interest. So the Christian theory claims that societies without allegiance to the Intelligent and Benevolent Designer will inevitably lose the foundation of morality and succumb to the temptation to kill all enemies of the self (as it happened in the 20th century genocides and mass murders of millions). But the Christian theory also claims that the Intelligent Designer is not only intelligent, but also Benevolent—unselfish (*Agape*) Love itself. And this benevolent Love became visible in Jesus of Nazareth. And Jesus demonstrated the benevolence, Love and unselfishness of God by offering his life for his enemies (Romans 5:7-8). He forgave his executioners and taught his disciples to do the same (e.g., Matthew 5:44-48 and Luke 23:34 and Acts 7:60). The Christian theory claims that this sacrifice of Jesus (and his resurrection) was the spark that started Jerusalem "on fire" with *agape* love (Acts 2:42-47 and 4:32-35). And 300 years later, the whole Roman Empire, had been infused with unselfish Love. The Jesus Movement conquered the whole Roman empire in 313 A.D. without a single sword being drawn.[351] The Jesus Movement continues to be a major force in the world today as the largest religion in the world with more than 30% of the world population claiming membership.[352] Of course, not all who claim membership are unselfish, but the moral predictions above (in chapter 6) offer some clear evidence that the movement continues to be a force for good (and that the Intelligent Designer-God exists and is benevolent).

The Fourth Proof for the Existence of God

The Moral Evidence from Natural Law and Conscience

Francis Collins, head of the team that mapped the human genome, admits that there is a "gap" in scientific knowledge of how life began:

> But how did self-replicating organisms arise in the first place? It is fair to say that at the present time, we simply do not know.[353]

But Collins believes that sooner or later, this gap in scientific knowledge will be explained, so the theist should not base his faith on it:

> There are good reasons to believe in God, including the existence of mathematical principles and order in creation. They are positive reasons, based on knowledge, rather than

default assumptions, based on (a temporary) lack of knowledge.

In summary, while the question of the origin of life is a fascinating one, and the inability of modern science to develop a statistically probable mechanism is intriguing, this is not the place for a thoughtful person to wager his faith.[354]

Francis Collins evolved from atheist to Christian theist, but the biggest influence on his faith came not from science, but from C. S. Lewis and from the existence of the conscience and natural moral law. This is the fourth argument for the existence of God.

If the Law of Human Nature cannot be explained away as cultural artifact or evolutionary biproduct, then how can we account for its presence? There is truly something unusual going on here. To quote [C.S.] Lewis, "If there was a controlling power outside the universe, it could not show itself to us as one of the facts inside the universe—no more than the architect of a house could actually be a wall or staircase or fireplace in that house. The only way in which we could expect it to show itself would be inside ourselves as an influence or a command trying to get us to behave in a certain way. And that is just what we do find inside ourselves. Surely this ought to arouse our suspicions?"

Encountering this argument at age twenty-six, I was stunned by its logic.[355]

Natural Moral Law

The very existence of conscience and the natural moral law is evidence for the existence of God. We have seen above that conscience is the voice of God and that without God, there is no voice of conscience, no guilt to motivate us to do the good and avoid evil. If it weren't for the existence of conscience, the Jesus movement might not have been able to conquer the Roman Empire without a sword, slavery might not have been abolished, the non-violent Gandhi movement might not have gained Indian independence and the non-violent civil rights movement of Martin Luther King might not have succeeded. These great movements relied on the existence of conscience in the hearts of people. And without a benevolent God, there is no foundation for altruism—no motivation to be unselfish. As Collins states it,

> "Agape, or selfless altruism, presents a major challenge for the evolutionist... It cannot be accounted for by the drive of individual selfish genes to perpetuate themselves."[356]

And there can be no natural moral law without the Intelligent Designer of all natural laws. There are natural moral laws just as there are natural physical laws. And just as we have found with physical laws, so also we have found with natural moral law, there is a significant amount of agreement on what the laws are in many cultures throughout the world and the laws are surprisingly Anthropic (human-friendly).

> What we have here is very peculiar: the con-
> cept of right and wrong appears to be universal
> among all members of the human species
> (though its application may result in wildly dif-
> ferent outcomes). It thus seems to be a phe-
> nomenon approaching that of a law, like the law
> of gravitation or of special relativity.[357]

The founding fathers of the USA appealed to this universal natural law in their Declaration of Independence:

> "...the separate and equal station to which the
> Laws of Nature and of Nature's God entitle
> them...We hold these truths to be self-evident,
> that all men are created equal, that they are
> endowed by their Creator with certain unalien-
> able Rights, that among these are Life, Liberty
> and the pursuit of Happiness."[358]

It did not occur to the founders that appealing to human rights as God-given was an endorsement of a particular religion—belief in the Intelligent Designer is virtually universal, regardless of religion, and the belief that human rights are God-given frees us from the tyranny of a dictator and the tyranny of the majority. Thank God and our forefathers for the First amendment freedom of religion and for the whole Bill of Rights.

Natural Law points to the existence of the Intelligent Designer in two ways: first, there is no foundation for morality or altruism without the Intelligent Designer (Remember Dostoevsky's claim); secondly, there is evidence of order, design and benevolence in the natural laws themselves. Let's look at some key examples. Some Atheists are protesting the many depictions of the Ten Commandments on government property because they claim they are an endorsement of a particular religion, contrary to the First Amendment of the Constitution. Which religion is being endorsed? Judaism? Christianity? Or Islam? All three religions accept the prophecy of Moses the lawgiver (Surah 19:51-53 in the *Quran*) and these three religions alone account for 55% of the world's population[359] and 75% of the population of the USA.[360] The Ten Commandments do not endorse a particular religion nor even these three religions—they encode some of the most important values and laws that can be found in virtually every culture—outlawing the taking of someone's life, the stealing of someone's spouse or the stealing of the property of another person. Add to these the basic law against perjury by witnesses in trials and you have the fundamental Natural Laws of virtually any culture in the world. These laws are covered by six of the ten commandments. Add to these three commandments respecting the Intelligent Designer-God and the fourth, honoring parents, and the Decalogue is virtually complete.

For centuries, the Law of Moses was respected as the oldest documented version of Natural Law. However, archaeologists uncovered the Code of Hammurabi in 1901, dating about 400 years before Moses.[361] There are 282 laws in the Code[362] as compared to 613 in the Laws of Moses.[363] Most of these laws served to fine-tune the Law of Talion ("an eye for an eye and a tooth for a tooth")[364] in a way similar to the Law of Moses (Leviticus 24:17-20). Both codes served to temper the revenge of vigilantes who tended to take two eyes for one or all teeth for one—codes measured the damages of law-breakers and proportionately meted out punishment in a relatively objective manner. Of course, neither of these codes were perfect renditions of the Natural Law, so they had to undergo centuries of moral reasoning, cultural evolution and even revolutions[365]—to get where we are today. This is no different than the evolution that has occurred in science since the very primitive science of that era (1300-1700 B.C.). The understanding of Natural Laws and Physical Laws continue to evolve today. That the ancient understanding is so different than contemporary understanding is not a sign that all truth is relative—"relativism", as many people would have it. Rather it is evidence of the progress of cultural evolution that continues the natural selection of improved ideas and understandings of science and ethics.

We can imagine the beginning of human understanding of Natural Law. The first intelligent humans somehow acted in a selfish way against the other—the "original sin" (Genesis 3:6-7). One of earliest sins was murder (Genesis 4:8). Murders often were committed in battles over possessions. Man's most valuable "possession" was the woman—many murders probably came from mortal battles over women. The prohibition of murder probably became the first natural law. Another one of the first natural laws probably evolved from the human experience of childbirth numbers—male and female babies were born in approximately equal numbers. This meant that at puberty, there should have been one woman for each man— the natural law of monogamy. This natural law of monogamy was frequently broken by strong and greedy males who took more than their share of women. Also, warfare and murder took a disproportionate toll on the male population—many ancient tribes had many more women survivors than men. This distorted the intelligent design of the Natural Law and enabled the practice of polygamy. There weren't enough men to go around, so men needed to mate with more than one woman. In the evolution of cultures, the disproportion of men to women eventually became more balanced (and natural) and monogamy was recognized as the natural law in most cultures.

Another very ancient understanding of Natural Law centered around childbirth—there is an intrinsic connection in the intelligent design of human beings between the sex act and childbirth. Sex and pregnancy are intrinsically and naturally related. The Intelligent Designer linked these two realities together, apparently to ensure reproduction and the perpetuation of the human race. Imagine the human situation without this connection. What would be the motivation for getting pregnant? Without the sex drive, there probably would not have been enough pregnancies to maintain the human species—the human race might have died out for lack of reproduction. Our contemporary culture has become infatuated with the many ways that humans can separate reproduction from sex acts. Homosexuality, anal and oral sex, the condom, the Intra-Uterine Device (IUD), In Vitro Fertilization (IVF), cloning, abortion and "the Pill" are among the many ways that our "culture of death"[366] separates sex, marriage and reproduction.[367] In fact, the modern innovation of the birth control pill has changed sex into an act of recreation without reproduction. Some European Countries are currently experiencing the negative consequences of artificial birth control—childbirth rates less than the replacement number leading to a smaller population. This artificial

distortion of the population profile is leading to a disproportion in the ratio of workers to retirees—there aren't enough
workers to support the retirement costs of retirees.[368] Many
economies are borrowing money to cover costs and incur-
ring national debts that are at dangerous levels. Even in the
US where the replacement rate is about even, the national
debt is more than 20 trillion dollars, equal to an individual
debt of more than $50,000 owed by every man, woman and
child. The consequences of the natural law being violated in
the use of artificial birth control are enormous and we have
only begun to experience the negative effects of the sexual
revolution. The negative consequences of the birth control
pill, the artificial separation of sex and reproduction, and the
sexual revolution were predicted by Pope Paul VI in his controversial encyclical, *Humani Vitae*.[369]

It is interesting to note that the Intelligent Designer has
programmed in the human body not only the connection
between sex and reproduction, but also four forms of natural birth control. The latency period prior to puberty offers a
natural protection from pregnancy in girls whose bodies are
not ready for it. Secondly, the woman's body is programmed
to stop ovulation at around 50 years old—menopause—pro-
tecting older women from the stress of pregnancy, childbirth
and nursing. Third, the woman's body is designed to pause
ovulation during the nursing stage of the infant, naturally
separating pregnancies by one, two or even three years.[370]
Fourthly, the monthly cycle of menstruation includes only
about 2 or 3 days of fertility during ovulation (1-day survival for the egg and 3 days for the sperm) making most of
the month infertile. This latter form of natural birth control
has recently been enhanced by significant discoveries of

technology for Natural Family Planning (NFP), making the natural methods at least as successful as the Birth Control Pill. NFP classes teach women the natural signs of ovulation including changes in the cervical mucous and temperature. Now pharmacies even have urine test strips (similar to pregnancy test strips) that indicate the day of ovulation. And the natural methods have none of the dangerous side-effects of the artificial methods.

Speaking of menopause, the evolutionists have no answer why this infertility in older women has been naturally selected.[371] Natural selection tends to favor fertility over infertility. How did menopause survive natural selection? Theists have an answer. Why not accept menopause as a gift of the Benevolent Designer for older women to get relief of the burdens of pregnancy and labor? Here is one period in a woman's life where natural infertility enables her to focus on the marital union and sexual intimacy without reproduction responsibilities. It is a mystery to the evolutionists as to why the human female is the only mammal that experiences menopause.[372] Thank God for the benevolent design of infertility for older women. Evolutionists are also baffled as to why women experience orgasm. Orgasm is rare among mammals (most female animals experience "heat" but not orgasm) and the female orgasm is unnecessary for reproduction.[373] In fact, the human female can experience orgasms whether she is fertile or not. What baffles the evolutionist makes common sense if there is a Benevolent Designer-God—the Benevolent Creator seems to have created orgasm in women to strengthen marriage and to perhaps give the woman a foretaste of the heavenly ecstasy of union with God.[374]

Another mystery of evolution is the phenomenon of inbreeding—closely related sexual couples tend to produce a much higher rate of genetic mutations, diseases and deformities than unrelated couples.[375] This phenomenon in which the genes of one partner are too much alike the genes of the other partner is confusing to evolution theory where natural selection favors fertility. It is also confusing to theorists of natural law—why would the Intelligent Designer program genetic problems with incest? There seems to be some reason why diversity in the genes of fathers and mothers is favored and incest is penalized. (Perhaps this is another natural incentive for altruism—loving non-blood-related persons?) Whatever the reason, the Natural Law prohibiting incest is virtually universal among the cultures of the world.

There also seems to be another incentive for monogamy and a natural penalty for promiscuity built into Natural Law. Sexually transmitted diseases (STDs) have accompanied sexual promiscuity for centuries. The Columbus crews that discovered the New World also contracted Syphilis and exported it to Europe.[376] The discovery of penicillin in the 20th century brought a cure for the two known STDs prior to the Sexual Revolution—syphilis and gonorrhea. But the sexual revolution of the 1960's caused epidemic of STDs previously unknown. By the turn of the millennium, STDs numbered more than 25, some of which are incurable.[377] The 1980's brought on the HIV–AIDS epidemic, killing millions.[378] In spite of the apparent design built into the Natural Law favoring marriage and monogamy and punishing promiscuity, the Sexual Revolution continues its blind direction toward disease and destruction. Two many in the millennial generation continue to believe in "relativism" instead of natural law and are not learning lessons from the failures of the "baby boomers".[379] There are epidemics of STDs on every college campus—college students are not surprised that they will get some form of STD sometime in their careers.[380] Instead of believing in and following the design of natural law, they put their faith in modern medicine to avoid the natural consequences of the sexual revolution. They are treating the symptoms rather than the disease.

United Nations Universal Declaration of Human Rights

Much of the Natural Law was uncovered in the Code of Hammurabi (262 laws) and much more of it was uncovered in the Law of Moses (613 laws). This does not mean that there was agreement in all of the details among all these laws—it does mean that there was agreement on many of the core values and in many of the details. The core values are similar and they are reflected at the center of the Ten Commandments—the values of human life, marriage, property and honesty: "you shall not murder; you shall not commit adultery; you shall not steal; you shall not commit perjury" (Exodus 20:13-16). Over the centuries, the understanding of Natural Law has been refined (in spite of the great diversity of nations, cultures and religions) by a process of Natural Selection. The Magna Carta[381] was a breakthrough in the definition of Natural Law in the 13th century England. The US Declaration of Independence was a breakthrough in the definition of Natural Law in the 18th century. But the greatest achievement in the definition of Natural Law came in 1948 from the United Nations in their "Universal Declaration of Human Rights".[382] This was also the greatest achievement (and one of the earliest) of the United Nations General Assembly. It is the greatest consensus on the planet regarding the Natural Law—48 nations voted in favor, none against (though 10 abstained).[383] There was no mention of the Intelligent Designer in the UN Declaration ("Nature's God" in the US Declaration of Independence), but there is an assumption that there is a design in natural law (and there-fore an assumption that there is a Designer?). These rights do not come from governments but from a Higher Power.

There didn't have to be a design in Natural Law. And there didn't have to be physical laws, either. The universe could have been nothing but random events with no order or consis-tency—and no possibility of science. (Remember Einstein's claim.)[384] Or there could have been physical laws without moral laws built into the universe. If there were no design in Natural Law, the law of Natural Selection of the most pow-erful individuals would rule—the survival of the fittest and "might makes right". The state of affairs on planet earth would resemble the Wild West or Big City Gangland—the reign of narcissism. In the 20th century the Wild West and Gangland warfare went global in the two world wars and the purging of millions of undesirables by "gang leaders" the likes of Hitler, Stalin and Mao Zedong. As we have seen above (in chapter 6), the mass murders of these millions was a confirmation of the prediction of what would happen if there were no belief in the Intelligent Designer of Natural Law.[385] Now we can also claim that the evolution of natural law itself, culminating in the agreement in the United Nations on the Universal Declaration of Human Rights, could not have happened without design existing in the Natural Law—there would be no natural law.

The very existence of Natural Law design points to the existence of the Intelligent Designer-God.

This Natural Law argument for the existence of God could produce a whole book by itself. We have numbered above several predictions that have been tested in the real world that confirm the hypothesis of an Intelligent Designer of Natural Law. There are hundreds of studies that have been documented on the Anthropic quality of religion—the positive benefits to human life from the practice of religion—for example, in *The Handbook of Religion and Health*.[386] The irony is that many people are not aware of or are not persuaded by the evidence, so they continue their lives without the benefit of belief in God, the very thing that could increase their well-being. And the next step in the process of evolution awaits a consensus on this faith.

God Speaks

The Book of Job has 42 chapters. In the first 2 chapters we read of the Patience of Jobe. In the subsequent chapters, Jobe became frustrated at the unfairness of God—Jobe Syndrome had set in. The three friends of Jobe all try to defend God against the accusations of Jobe that God is unfair. In doing so, they attack the virtue of Jobe, saying he must have done something to deserve God's punishment. In all the arguments between Jobe and his friends, God is silent. Finally, in the final chapters 38, 39, 40, and 41, God speaks. The following epilogue is a modern scientific version of what I believe God was saying to Jobe in those four chapters.

Jobe,

Who are you to question My intentions when I made the universe? You have no idea what My intentions are. Now, stand up like a man and I will ask you some questions and you give me the answers if you are so smart! Since you are so smart, tell me—where were you when I made the universe? Why didn't you give me your great ideas while I was doing creation? Now that you are here, why don't you create a better universe from nothing? Do you even know how huge the universe is?

Can you imagine how fast is the speed of light—186,000 miles per second? (What took you so long (300,000 years) to measure it?) Do you know that the light waves from millions of stars at the far end of the universe have not yet reached us—even though they are traveling at the speed of light? And you think you can measure the universe! It took you 300,000 years to discover that Mother Earth revolves around the sun and not the reverse. What holds her in orbit? Do you realize that Mother Earth is in an orbit perfectly distant from Brother Sun to have climates friendly to human life—no other planet that you know of has these climates. And even if they did, would they have a perfect atmosphere of Nitrogen, Oxygen and Carbon Dioxide—molecules friendly to human life? As far as you know, no other planet has this balance.

Do you realize how lucky you are to have been born on this planet? And how come it took you so long to measure the gravitational constant? Do you know how precisely I had to make this constant in order to prevent the earth from shooting out of orbit or collapsing into a black hole long ago?[387] Do you know how precisely I had to balance the forces of gravity, electromagnetism and the nuclear forces in order to enable the existence of Carbon atoms, Oxygen atoms and Nitrogen atoms?[388] Do you realize how lucky you are to live on Mother Earth? Do you realize how many times in a row you have won the lottery of life? You have had only one chance in 10—with 120 zeros after it—to even exist![389] That is equal to you winning the lottery more than 100 days in a row! Do you know how "truly astonishing" is the delicate balance of the precise values of the forces of gravity and electromagnetism? Without this precise balance, "all stars would be red dwarfs" or "blue giants".[390] Then what planet would you live on? Do you understand what nuclear resonance is? If the nuclear resonance levels of carbon, oxygen, helium and beryllium had not been precisely balanced in an "extremely remote coincidence... then carbon would be extremely rare, and carbon-based life forms would not have emerged."[391] This discovery, more than anything else, converted an atheist physicist (Fred Hoyle) to believe in a "super-calculating Intellect"[392] (that's Me). Why do you doubt?

Have you figured out how I brought organic chemicals to life? Why not? You have had 300,000 years to discover how I made a single living cell and you still have not been able to duplicate this process in the laboratory. What is taking you so long? How can you do a better job of creating the universe if you can't bring chemicals to life? You have figured out how I used mutation and natural selection to create the thousands of different plants, animals and fish and birds—and then you leave me out of it! You claim that you don't need me as a source of life—how arrogant! Or even if you give me credit for creating the universe, you deny that you need me as a sustainer of life or a force for benevolence overcoming selfishness. How arrogant! You are celebrating the age of the computer and the internet, but I produced the human brain 300,000 years ago and your computers and robots cannot come even close to matching the feats of human beings. And how do you explain this wonderful process of evolution toward complexity, order and intelligence in the face of the law of Entropy—the force toward chaos and disorder? You claim that I do not exist or if I do exist, I am silent—you say I have never spoken to you—I do not answer you. Can you blame me that you didn't discover my DNA language until 1953?[393] I wrote the whole encyclopedia of books of instructions on how to create every cell in the universe—I wrote these instructions in the nucleus of each cell—in My language—DNA.[394] You finally learned my instructions on how to create a human being in 2003—it took 2000 scientists years to do this![395] I am so glad you finally learned My language—the language of creation—implanted in every living cell in the universe. Don't forget Who wrote it!

It wasn't only the language of creation that I have been speaking to you—I have been speaking to each one of you ever since the evolution of human beings—in your own language—in your conscience. Conscience produces those thoughts that come into your mind that have a moral theme. I have been telling you how to make moral decisions ever since you came into the age of reason (from about 7 years old). When you thought those thoughts—"You should do this" or "Don't do that"—I was speaking to you. Sometimes, after some people have ignored My voice repeatedly, they lost my thoughts altogether—they cannot hear My voice anymore. This is a tragic death of conscience. But I keep trying to coach you to happiness, whether you listen to Me or not. And when you do not listen to me, you act selfishly and people get hurt— you and someone(s) else. Yet I keep trying to stop you from hurting yourself and others.

What would you do to stop evil? Would you eliminate free will? I gave up My control over human decisions so that they could be free to love—I wish they would love—but many choose selfishness. If you eliminate free will you would eliminate human beings—do you really want a world without humans? Without you? And if I eliminated only the people who have sinned, how many people would be left? Would you be left?

Have you never sinned? You do remember that I tried this solution with Noah—it didn't work. (Genesis 9:20-21)

I have chosen to give up My control over peoples' decisions so that they can love. But I have created moral laws that are just as natural and just as unbreakable as the laws of physics—natural selection will eventually eliminate the individuals and the cultures that break them regularly. Eventually, all the evildoers that live by narcissism and who are addicted to the worship of themselves will become stuck in hell. There is a connection between loving and being loved, sacrifice and happiness, religion and health—eventually, those who let go of their lives will receive eternal life. Those who act unselfishly will receive a great reward. Those who "live in love will live in Me and I will live in them" (1 John 4:16). Can you come up with a better design for morality in your universe? Tell me about it. I am sorry that My universe includes pain and death. I am so sorry that there are terrible accidents in my world. I am sorry that people choose to sin and hurt people with their gift of free will. If you can come up with a way to sort out evildoers (who will never reform) from good people who sinned but have changed or will change their ways, I will be among the first to praise you. And then you won't need Me to eliminate sin. Good luck on your noble plan!

It takes Almighty power to create a universe and to sustain it. You have discovered the immensity of nuclear power that I have compressed in every atom of the universe. I created that power. The kinetic energy of the asteroids hurtling through space at thousands of miles per hour is greater than the energy of many nuclear bombs. If one large asteroid collided with planet earth, it would cause the end of the world for you humans. I created the asteroids. Can you even imagine that kind of power? Can you imagine the power of the force of gravity to hold planet earth in orbit around the sun? That power of gravity is so strong that it can condense stars and planets into a single point in space smaller than a pinhead— infinite gravity—this is what we call a "black hole". I created black holes. Can you even imagine doing such a thing?

> And Job answered God.
> ² I know that you can do all things,
> and that no purpose of yours can be hindered.
> ³ "Who is this who obscures counsel with ignorance?"
> I have spoken but did not understand;
> things too marvelous for me, which I
> did not know…
> ⁵ By hearsay I had heard of you,
> but now my eye has seen you.
> ⁶ Therefore I disown what I have said,
> and repent in dust and ashes. (Job 42:2-6)

Jobe received a glimpse of the beautiful side of the tapestry of life—now he knows that there are reasons why the backside of the tapestry is so chaotic and obscure. And knowing that there is a frontside of the tapestry that reveals meaning and purpose to the whole, comforted Jobe in his time of depression—his "dark night of the soul".[396] Jobe could now go on. And now that we have a glimpse of the other side of the tapestry, we, too, can go on. We can believe there is light at the end of the tunnel. We can get through the "dark night" of our grief and pain and sadness. We can find meaning and design and purpose in spite of the chaos of life and the fear of death. We can heal from Jobe Syndrome. Thanks be to God.

Everything in this book should be good news to the believer—and perhaps bad news for the unbeliever. It reminds us of "Pascal's Wager".[397] Blaise Pascal was a seventeenth century philosopher, mathematician and physicist. He is famous for his "wager"—he challenges all of us to bet our lives on whether or not God exists. He suggests that only a fool would bet against the existence of God.

> The wise decision is to wager that God exists, since "If you gain, you gain all; if you lose, you lose nothing", meaning one can gain eternal life if God exists, but if not, one will be no worse off in death than if one had not believed. On the other hand, if you bet against God, win or lose, you either gain nothing or lose everything."

Each of us must choose between belief in God or unbelief. Pascal challenges us to use our common sense—believers have everything to gain and nothing to lose.

Endnotes

1   https://www.dailywire.com/news/god-help-us-atheism-beco-mes-largest-religion-us-michael-j-knowles

2   www.gss.norc.org 2018 data from the National Opinion Research Center, University of Chicago.

3   www.ericmetaxas.com/media/articles/science-increasingly-makes-case-god/

4   Ibid.

5   Ibid.

6   *Ann Arbor News*, Ann Arbor, MI. March 7, 2006 (front page story by Geoff Larcom)

7   https://www.dailywire.com/news/watch-renowned-yale-prof-leaves-darwinism-says-amanda-prestigiacomo

8   Teilhard de Chardin (1948/1955/1959). *The Phenomenon of Man*. NY: Harper and Row.

9   John of the Cross (2003). *Dark Night of the Soul*. Westminster, Maryland: The Newman Press.

10 Note that I have changed the usual spelling of Jobe throughout my book. I believe the usual spelling is problematic because in print, it can look like the name of our work—our "job". My spelling is intended to avoid the possible confusion between "Jobe" and "job".

11 https://www.facebook.com/BishopRobertBarron/videos/looking-for-the-nones-bishop-barron-at-cultures-of-forma-tion-conference-notre-da/1689914547714332/

Notes to Chapter One: Jobe Syndrome

12   Holy Cross Children's Services (HCCS) is a Catholic social services agency serving abused, abandoned and delinquent and otherwise at-risk children and their families in Michigan with residential treatment, day treatment, foster care, independent living and in-home services. The research in this book comes from the long term (one year) residential treatment programs at five campuses serving primarily delinquent boys and girls from 12–18 years of age. The largest campus was Boysville, located in Clinton, Michigan.

13   The names of these persons have been changed to conceal their identity.

14   Philip Yancey, *Disappointment With God*, Harper Collins Publishers (New York: 1988); Cf. his earlier work on pain: *Where is God When It Hurts?*, Zondervan Publishing House (Grand Rapids, MI: 1977)

15   *Disappointment With God, op. cit.*, p. 30.

16   Harold Kushner, *When Bad Things Happen To Good People*, Avon Books (New York: 1981)

17   Ibid., p. 42-43.

18   Ibid., p.50.

19   Robert Cardinal Sarah (2017). *The Power of Silence*. San Francisco: Ignatius Press. P.145.

20   Ibid., p.91.

21   Ibid., p.91.

22   Ibid., p.150.

23   Ibid., p.147.

24   *Catechism of the Catholic Church* (1994). Washington D.C.: United States Catholic Conference. Para. 311.

25   Several similar "Letters to God" can be found in Appendix A, PAGE 217

26 Kenneth Pargament, Brian Zinnbauer, Allie Scott, Eric Butter, Jill Zerowin, and Patricia Stanik, "Red Flags and Religious Coping: Identifying Some Religious Warning Signs Among People in Crisis", *Journal of Clinical Psychology,* Vol. 54, No. 1 (1998), p. 86; this corroborates the findings of Berg, *et al.* that mental health patients who believe that "God/Life has treated me unfairly" require significantly more medical treatment than the others (p.362). Berg's "Spiritual Injury Scale" seems to be a good measure of Job's Syndrome symptoms. Park, Cohen and Herb, conclude that denomination or Religion may be a key variable in the coping ability during certain life stresses ("Intrinsic Religiousness and Religious Coping as Life Stress Moderators for Catholics Versus Protestants", *Journal of Personality and Social Psychology*, Vol. 59, No. 3, p. 573). Pargament (1997) *The Psychology of Religion and Coping.* NY: The Guilford Press. (E.g., pp. 318ff).

27 See appendix B, PAGE 221 for the whole protocol. Cf. James Kok, *The Pastoral Counseling Treatment Planner*, John Wiley and Sons, Inc. NY (1998) where he has a protocol for treating "Anger at God".

28 James R. Kok and Arthur E. Jongsma, Jr., *The Pastoral Counseling Treatment Planner*, John Wiley and Sons, Inc. (New York, 1998), p. 15, where "long-term goal" #2 involves "Forgiving God and returning to a personal relationship with him".

29 Francis McNutt, *Healing*, Ave Maria Press (Notre Dame: 1978) p. 226.

30 Garth Brooks, Pat Alger, Larry Bastian (1990). *Unanswered Prayers*. CD from the album *No Fences.* Capitol Nashville.

31 Philip Yancey, *Where Is God When It Hurts?* Zondervan (Grand Rapids: 1977); Cf. Kushner, *op. cit.,* p. 18, where he rejects the concept of Thornton Wilder's "tapestry" of life, whose front side is a beautiful piece of art, while its back side, the only side

visible to us humans, is an apparent hodgepodge of colored threads. The tapestry is a metaphor offering meaning and purpose to the many difficult events of life that seem meaningless. (See the Tapestry picture in chapter five.)

32   Kushner, *op. cit.*, pp. 89f. Kushner's thesis is basically that God is not to be blamed for all the hurts people experience in the world, so he teaches us why we don't need to be angry at God. However, he offers us good interventions for Job who "needed friends who would permit him to be angry". Cf. Linn, *et. al.*, *op. cit.*, p. 48: "Sometimes the one we need to confront is God. Give myself permission to be angry at God, and share it with God and others." Cf. Padovani, *Healing Wounded Emotions*, Twenty Third Publications (Mystic, CT: 1987). Cf. Walter Bruggeman (2001). *Spirituality of the Psalms.* Fortress Press.

33   James Pennebaker, "Writing About Emotional Experiences As a Therapeutic Process", *Psychological Science,* Volumn 8, No. 3 (May, 1997): Pennebaker documents the physical and emotional health outcomes of "venting" about traumatic experiences whether verbally or in writing.

34   James Kok, *op. cit.,* p. 17. Kok includes interventions including the encouraging of the counselee to pray these psalms. However, Kok's interventions fail to prescribe that the counselor pray these psalms together with the counselee, an intervention I have found to be powerful. Note also above, the innovation that has the clients compose and pray their own psalms of lament.

35   Not her real name.

36   James Kok, op. cit., p. 16: "Therapeutic Interventions... 2. Ask to hear the whole story... 3. Exhibit an attitude of warmth... 4. Explore the feelings of hurt... 5. Express empathy strongly... 7. Explore feelings of abandonment by God..."

37   Charles Taylor, *The Skilled Pastor*, Fortress Press (Minneapolis: 1991), p. 55.

Notes to Chapter Two: Metaphysics and Physics

38   Paul Vitz (2013). *Faith of the Fatherless: The Psychology of Atheism*. San Francisco: Ignatius Press. P. 29.

39   Ibid., p.166-169. Vitz changed his views on cultural evolution because of evidence that even some primitive cultures were monotheistic.

40   Anthony Flew (1966), *Body, Mind and Death*. London: Macmillan.

41   Kuhn, Thomas (1996) *The Structure of Scientific Revolutions*. University of Chicago Press.

42   Newton's law of universal gravitation. Retrieved from en.m.wikipedia.org: the gravitational force is directly proportional to the product of the masses of the two particles and inversely proportional to the square of the distance between their centers: ($F=G(m')(m'')$ /r squared where F= the force of gravity, G = gravitational constant, m' = mass of object 1 and m'' = mass of object 2 and r = distance between objects).

43   Robert Spitzer (2010). *New Proofs for the Existence of God*. Grand Rapids, MI: William Eerdmans

44   Who discovered electrons, protons and neutrons? Retrieved from scienceline.ucsb.edu

45   What is Atomic Weight? Retrieved from thoughtco.com

46   Ibid.

47   Quark. Retrieved from en.m.wikipedia.org

48   Strong interaction. Retrieved from en.m.wikipedia.org

49   Scientific method. Retrieved from en.m.wikipedia.org

50   Michael Behe agrees with this definition of science. Michael Behe (1996/2006). *Darwin's Black Box*. NY: Simon and Schuster. P.238.

51   Johannes Kepler. Retrieved from en.m.wikipedia.org

52   Teilhard de Chardin (1948/1955/1959). *The Phenomenon of Man*. NY: Harper and Row. Biologist St. George Mivart was a Catholic evolutionist. Joshua Moritz (Fall 2019). Science Vs. Religion. *Aspire* Volume 1, p.32.

53   Georges Lemaitre. Retrieved from en.m.wikipedia.org

54   Michael Behe (2006). *Darwin's Black Box*. NY: Simon and Schuster. P.245.

55   Redshift. Retrieved from en.m.wikipedia.org

56   Stephen Hawking (2010). *The Grand Design.* NY: Bantam Books. (He died on March 14, 2018)

57   Stephen Hawking (1988). *A Brief History of Time*. NY: Bantam Books.

58   Stephen Hawking (1988). *A Brief History of Time*: *From the Big Bang to Black Holes*. NY: Bantam Books.

59   Survival of the Fittest. Retrieved from en.m.wikipedia.

60   Absolute zero. Retrieved from en.m.wikipedia.

61   Thaxton, Bradley and Olson (1984) *The Mystery of Life's Origin*. Dallas: Lewis and Stanley. P. 144: "A mere appeal to open system thermodynamics does little good."

62   Michael Behe (1996/2006). *Darwin's Black Box*. NY: Simon and Schuster. Pp.42-43.

63   Ibid., p. 211.

64   Biology: Cell Structure. Retrieved from www.youtube.com.

65   Michael Behe (2006). *Darwin's Black Box*. NY: Simon and Schuster. P. 73. Cf. Thaxton, Bradley and Olson (1984) *The Mystery of Life's Origin*. Dallas: Lewis and Stanley. P.127.

66   Michael Behe (2006). *Darwin's Black Box*. NY: Simon and Schuster. P.193

67   Ibid., p.193.

68   Ibid., p.233.

69   Ibid., p.252

70   Ibid., p. 255.

71   Ibid., p.197

72   Ibid., p.239

73   Ibid., p.5

74   Ibid., p.168

75   Ibid., pp. 168-169

76   Ibid., p.171

77   Francis Collins (2006). *The Language of God.* NY: Simon and Schuster. P. 93.

78   Ibid.

79   Stephen Meyer (2009). *Signature in the Cell: DNA and the Evidence for Intelligent Design.* NY: Harper-Collins. (P. 26). Cf. Thaxton, Bradley and Olson (1984) *The Mystery of Life's Origin.* Dallas: Lewis and Stanley. "It cannot be denied that the "pure chance" view of the origin of life is a position of extreme faith". (P.5)

80   Stephen Hawking (1988). *A Brief History of Time.* NY: Bantam Books. P. 152. Cf. Thaxton, Bradley and Olsen (1984) *The Mystery of Life's Origin.* Dallas: Lewis and Stanley. P.118 and p. 121.

81   Stephen Hawking (2010). *The Grand Design.* NY: Bantam Books. PP. 8-9,136-7, 136-144, 163-165, 185. (No mention of Thermodynamics or Entropy in this book.)

82   Stephen Hawking (1988). *A Brief History of Time.* P. 152

83   Stephen Hawking (2010). *The Grand Design.* P. 58, p. 117, p. 143, p. 181.

84   Retrieved from Hawking: Aliens may pose risks to Earth. nbc-news.com Cf. Francis Crick who believes that aliens brought the first living cells to earth in their rocket ship. Michael Behe (1996/2006). *Darwin's Black Box.* NY: Simon and Schuster. P.248.

85   Robert Spitzer (2010). *New Proofs for the Existence of God.* Grand Rapids, MI: William Eerdmans

86   Stephen Hawking (2010). *The Grand Design.* Pp. 103-104.

87   Primordial soup. Retrieved from en.m.wikipedia.org.

88 Stephen Hawking (1988). *A Brief History of Time*. Pp. 124-126. Or (2010). *The Grand Design*. Pp. 155, p. 159.

89 Robert Spitzer (2010). *New Proofs for the Existence of God*. Grand Rapids, MI: William Eerdmans

90 Stephen Hawking (1988). P. 56.

91 Schroedinger equation. Retrieved from http://hyperphysics. phy-astr.gsu.edu/hbase/quantum/schr.html

92 Uncertainty principle. Retrieved from en.m.wikipedia.org

93 Bohr model. Retrieved from https://en.wikipedia.org/wiki/ Bohr_model

94 Ibid.

95 Normal Distribution. Retrieved from en.m.wikipedia.org

96 Hausmann, Eugene (2004). Chaplain contacts improve treatment outcomes in residential programs for delinquent adolescents. *Journal of Pastoral Care and Counseling*. Vol. 58. No. 3. (Fall, 2004). Pp. 215-224.

97 Hausmann, Eugene and Mary Spooner (2009). Does Pastoral Counseling Work? A Pilot Study of Delinquent Boys. *Journal of Pastoral Care and Counseling*. Vol 63. No. 3,4 (Fall/ Winter, 2009).

98 Ibid.

99 Koenig, McCullough and Larson (2001) *The Handbook of Religion and Health*. NY: Oxford Press.

100 Ibid., page 325.

101 Robert Cardinal Sarah (2017). *The Power of Silence*. San Francisco: Ignatius Press. P. 90 where the atheist misinterprets God's "silence about catastrophes". Cf. Rabbi Harold Kushner (1981) *When Bad Things Happen to Good People*. NY: Random House. pp. 61-62.

Notes to Chapter Three: Miracles

102 Stephen Hawking (2010). *The Grand Design*. P. 181.

103   Larry Dossey (1993). *Healing Words: The Power of Prayer and the Practice of Medicine*. Harper San Francisco.

104   Herbert Benson (1996). *Timeless Healing*. NY: Simon and Schuster.

105   Larry Dossey (1993). *Healing Words*. NY: HarperCollins.

106   Harold Koenig (1999). *The Healing Power of Faith*. NY: Simon and Schuster. P. 27: "I recognize that research can neither prove nor disprove the reality of answered prayers or divine intercession."

107   Francis MacNutt (1974). *Healing*. Notre Dame: Ave Maria Press. P. 226.

108   List of saints canonized by Pope John Paul II. Retrieved from en.m.wikipedia.org. Cf. Fred Holye's claim that miracles no longer happen: Fred Hoyle (1983) *The Intelligent Universe*. London: Michael Joseph. (P.237-238).

109   Egg cell. Retrieved from en.m.wikipedia.org

110   Miracle of Life (1986). A NOVA series DVD. A Swedish Television Production in association with WGBH Boston. WGBH Education Foundation.

111   Retrieved from genome.gov (Search for human genome mapping complete)

112   Francis Collins (2000). The Language of God. Stephen Meyer (2009) Signature in the cell.

113   Roma Downey (2018). *Box of Butterflies*. NY: Howard Books. Pp. 193-195.

114   Black death. Retrieved from en.m.wikipedia.org

115   List of Deists. Retrieved from en.m.wikipedia.org

116   Thaxton, Bradley and Olson (1984) *The Mystery of Life's Origin*. Dallas: Lewis and Stanley. P. 144: "A mere appeal to open system thermodynamics does little good."

117   Actually, the proper category is an "Isolated system": Thaxton, Bradley and Olson (1984) *The Mystery of Life's Origin*. Dallas: Lewis and Stanley. P.117.

118   Paul Vitz (2013). Faith of the Fatherless. San Francisco: Ignatius Press. P. 78-80. For the emotional aspects of Dawkin's atheism.

119   Richard Dawkins (1989). *The Selfish Gene*. Oxford University Press.

120   Donald T. Campbell, On the Conflicts Between Biological and Social Evolution and Between Psychology and Moral Tradition. *Zygon*, volume 11, no. 3 (September 1976), pp. 197-198.

121   Ibid., pp.188-189.

Notes to Chapter Four: Brother Sun, Sister Moon

122   Canticle of the Sun. retrieved from https://en.wikipedia.org/wiki/Canticle_of_the_Sun#Text_and_translation

123   Stephen Meyer on Who made God? Stephen Meyer (2009). Pp. 388-389.

124   Lunar Rover. Retrieved from en.m.wikipedia.org.

125   Stephen Hawking (1988). *A Brief History of Time*. P. 145. Cf. Thaxton, Bradley and Olson (1984) *The Mystery of Life's Origin*. Dallas: Lewis and Stanley. P.113 and 116 and 118 and 121.

126   Stephen Hawking (1988). *A Brief History of Time*. Pp. 124-126. Stephen Hawking (2010). *The Grand Design*. P. 159

127   Stephen Hawking (1988). *A Brief History of Time*. Pp. 124-125.

128   Ibid., p. 126.

129   Ibid., p.127. Cf. Thaxton, Bradley and Olson (1984) *The Mystery of Life's Origin*. Dallas: Lewis and Stanley.P.201.

130   Stephen Hawking (1988). *A Brief History of Time*. p. 122

131   Ibid., pp. 140-141

132   ibid., p. 174

133   Ibid., p.175

134   Stephen Hawking (2010). *The Grand Design*. P. 58.

135   Ibid., p. 117.

136   Ibid., p. 119 and p. 143-144.

137 Ibid., p. 155. Fred Hoyle (1983) *The Intelligent Universe*. London: Michael Joseph. (Pp. 217-223) Hoyle is critical of the "anthropic principle" but he seems to be referring to it in its "weak form"; Hawking's description of the "strong form" of the anthropic principle would agree with Hoyle, I believe.

138 Stephen Hawking (2010). *The Grand Design*, pp. 162-163.

139 Ibid., p.163.

140 Ibid., p. 164.

141 Retrieved from Hawking: Aliens may pose risks to Earth. nbcnews.com

142 Stephen Hawking (2010). *The Grand Design*. P. 165.

143 Francis Collins (2006). *The Language of God*. NY: Simon and Schuster. Also, Stephen Meyer (2009). *Signature in the Cell*. NY: Harper-Collins.

144 Stephen Hawking (2010). *The Grand Design* (2010). P. 172.

145 Retrieved from Hawking: Aliens may pose risks to Earth. nbcnews.com

146 Stephen Hawking (2010). *The Grand Design*. P. 127.

147 Ibid., pp. 159-160. Cf. Fred Hoyle (1983). *The Intelligent Universe*. London: Michael Joseph. (pp.218-219).

148 Stephen Hawking (2010). *The Grand Design* p. 159.

149 Fred Hoyle (1983) *The Intelligent Universe*. NY: Holt, Reinhart and Winston.

150 Robert Spitzer (2010). *New Proofs for the Existence of God*. Grand Rapids, MI: William Eerdmans. P.73

151 Fred Hoyle (1981). *Engineering and Science*. Pasadena, CA: California Institute of Technology. Pp..8-12.

152 Stephen Meyer (2009). *Signature in the Cell*. p. 257. Fred Hoyle's version of the story (1983). *The Intelligent Universe*. London: Michael Joseph (p.19).

153 Robert Spitzer (2010). *New Proofs for the Existence of God*. Grand Rapids, MI: William Eerdmans. p.49.

154 Stephen Hawking, *A Brief History of Time*. P. 50.

155 Robert Spitzer (2010). *New Proofs for the Existence of God.* Pp. 49-50.

156 Ibid., p. 13.

157 Ibid., p.49, note 9.

158 Ibid., p. 48. Cf. Fred Hoyle (1983). *The Intelligent Universe.* London: Michael Joseph. (p. 168)

159 The Challenge of Solipsism. Retrieved from: www3.sympatico.ca.

160 Robert Spitzer., p. 56.

161 Ibid., p. 57.

162 Stephen Hawking (1988). P. 50.

163 Robert Spitzer. P. 59.

164 Ibid., p. 59.

165 Ibid., p. 60.

166 Ibid., p.61-62.

167 Ibid., p. 62.

168 Ibid., p. 63.

169 Ibid., p. 64.

170 Ibid., p. 45

Notes to Chapter 5: Mother Earth

171 Evolution of Cells. Retrieved from en.m.wikipedia.org.

172 Hadean age. Retrieved from en.m.wikipedia.org.

173 Harold Kushner (1981). *When Bad Things Happen to Good People.* NY: Random House. Pp. 20-22. Figure 1: Sassoferrato, Madonna and Child. The Catholic Company, 615 E. Westinghouse Blvd. Charlotte NC 28273.

174 Harold Kushner, op. cit., p. 59fff.

175 Ibid., p. 23.

176 Ibid., p. 94.

177 Cardinal Robert Sarah (2017). *The Power of Silence.* San Francisco: Ignatius Press. P. 92.

178 Ibid.

179   Natural Selection. Retrieved from en.m.wikipedia.org.

180   Ibid.

181   Fred Hoyle (1983). *The Intelligent Universe*. London: Michael Joseph. "Errors [in DNA copying] are much more likely to be harmful than beneficial." (p. 36)

182   Creation scientists like Grady McMurtry have found many other "gaps" in evolution theory and in the dating of planet earth—they argue for the "young earth" theory to make it compatible with Genesis 1. (www.creationworldview.org) Cf. Bob Duko (www.toptenproofs.com)

183   Synthetic biology. Retrieved from en.m.wikipedia.org. Thaxton, Bradley and Olson (1984) *The Mystery of Life's Origin*. Dallas: Lewis and Stanley. They count a total of "nineteen of the twenty proteinous amino acids, all five heterocyclic bases found in nucleic acids and several essential sugars..." (p.38)

184   Francis Collins (2006). *The Language of God*. NY: Simon and Schuster. P.93.

185   Robert Spitzer (2010). *New Proofs for the Existence of God*, p. 26, 29.

186   Ibid., p. 58.

187   Teilhard de Chardin, 1955. The English Edition, *Phenomenon of Man*, was first published in 1959. NY: Harper and Row.

188   Ibid., p. 29. The questionable orthodoxy of Teilhard has been ignored by recent popes who have cited his ideas: https://www.ncronline.org/news/pope-cites-teilhardian-vision-cosmos-living-host

189   Teilhard de Chardin, p.55.

190   Ibid., p.56. Thaxton, Bradley and Olson (1984) *The Mystery of Life's Origin*. Dallas: Lewis and Stanley. They call the "within" a "vital force (which had been held to be a kind of energy)" P. 13.

191   On the soul. Retrieved from en.m.wikipedia.org.

192   Teilhard de Chardin, pp. 58-59.

193   Ibid., p. 61.

194   Ibid., p. 73.

195   Hayflick Limit. Retrieved from en.m.wikipedia.org.

196   Francis Collins (2006). *The Language of God*. NY: Simon and Schuster. P. 131. Cf. Fred Hoyle (1983). *The Intelligent Universe*. London: Michael Joseph. "Errors [in DNA copying] are much more likely to be harmful than beneficial." (p. 36)

197   Existence of God. Retrieved from en.m.wikipedia.org

198   Francis Collins (2006). *The Language of God*. NY: Simon and Schuster.

199   Stephen Meyer (2009). *Signature in the Cell: DNA and the Evidence for Intelligent Design*. NY: Harper Collins.

200   Rosetta Stone. Retrieved from en.m.wikipedia.org.

201   Dolphin language. Retrieved from en.m.wikipedia.org.

202   Stephen Meyer (2009). *Signature in the Cell: DNA and the Evidence for Intelligent Design*. NY: Harper Collins. P.12

203   Francis Collins, (2006). *The Language of God*. NY: Simon and Schuster. p.113

204   Ibid. p.111

205   Ibid., p.123.

206   Ibid., p 246.

207   Miriam Michael Stimson. Retrieved from en.m.wikipedia.org.

208   Jun Tsuji (2004). *The Soul of DNA*. Coral Springs, FL: Lumina Press.

209   Ibid., p.113.

210   Ibid., p. 114.

211   Ibid., p. 121.

212   Ibid., p. 119.

213   Stephen Meyer (2004). "The origin of biological information and the higher taxonomic categories." *Proceedings of the Biological Society of Washington*. Volume 117 (2) (August 2004) Pp. 213-239.

214   Stephen Meyer (2009). *Signature in the Cell: DNA and the Evidence for Intelligent Design*. NY: Harper Collins. Pp. 1-2

215 Ibid., p. 4.

216 Ibid., p. 5.

217 Ibid., p. 26. Thaxton, Bradley and Olson (1984) *The Mystery of Life's Origin*. Dallas: Lewis and Stanley. Pp. 211-212. Cf. Fred Hoyle (1983). *The Intelligent Universe*. London: Michael Joseph. states "…the crucial issue of how the relevant genetic information originated in the first place… At some stage the genesis of the information must be explained." (p. 47).

218 Stephen Meyer. Op Cit. p. 85. Cf. Thaxton, Bradley and Olson (1984) *The Mystery of Life's Origin*. Dallas: Lewis and Stanley: "Information and entropy" p.131.

219 Stephen Meyer (2009). *Signature in the Cell: DNA and the Evidence for Intelligent Design*. NY: Harper Collins. p. 109. Thaxton, Bradley and Olson (1984) *The Mystery of Life's Origin*. Dallas: Lewis and Stanley. P.211f.

220 Stephen Meyer (2009). *Signature in the Cell: DNA and the Evidence for Intelligent Design*. NY: Harper Collins. P.110

221 Ibid., p. 142.

222 Ibid., p. 201.

223 Ibid., p. 203.

224 Ibid., p. 205.

225 Ibid., p. 208.

226 Ibid., p. 211.

227 Ibid., p. 219.

228 Ibid., pp. 239f

229 Ibid., p. 85. Cf. Fred Hoyle (1983). *The Intelligent Universe*. London: Michael Joseph (p.214): "…then we approach the ultimate cause instead of receding from it, the ultimate cause being a source of information, an intelligence, if you like, placed in the remote future…"

Notes to Chapter 6: Predictions from the Intelligent Design Hypothesis

230 Stephen Meyer (2009). *Signature in the Cell: DNA and the Evidence for Intelligent Design*. NY: Harper Collins. Pp. 495-496.

231 Ibid., p.494.

232 Ibid., pp. 496-497.

233 Ibid., p. 497.

234 Escherichia coli. Retrieved from en.m.wikipedia.org

235 Five ways (Aquinas). Retrieved from en.m.wikipedia.org

236 Big Bang. Retrieved from en.m.wikipedia.org

237 Stephen Hawking (2010), p. 119.

238 Fred Hoyle (1983). *The Intelligent Universe*. London: Michael Joseph. Where he claims "Life cannot have arisen by chance" (pp. 11-12 and 17-18). "No evidence for this huge jump in complexity has ever been found, nor in my opinion will it be." (p.18).

239 Teilhard de Chardin (1948/1955/1959). *The Phenomenon of Man*. NY: Harper and Row. P. 56.

240 Ibid., p.143.

241 Ibid., p. 142. Teilhard's prediction has come true in the writings of several contemporary scientists. E.g., Fred Hoyle (1983). *The Intelligent Universe*. London: Michael Joseph. (p.202 and 249). Robert Spitzer names at least seven prominent scientists who demonstrate "remarkable openness...to the prospect of supernatural design". (See note 153.) Add also Thaxton, Bradley and Olson (1984) *The Mystery of Life's Origin*. Dallas: Lewis and Stanley.

242 Teilhard de Chardin (1948/1955/1959). *The Phenomenon of Man*. NY: Harper and Row, p. 144.

243 Ibid., p. 181.

244 Ibid., pp. 182-183.

245 Ibid., p. 240.

246 Human Sacrifice. Retrieved from en.m.wikipedia.org.

247 Religious Populations. Retrieved from https://en.wikipedia. org/wiki/List_of_religious_populations

248 Paul Vitz (2013). *Faith of the Fatherless*. San Francisco: Ignatius Press. P. 34. For the emotional aspects of Nietzsche's atheism.

249 Friedrich Nietzsche. Retrieved from http://www.quotation-spage.com/quotes/Friedrich_Nietzsche/21.

250 Paul Vitz (2013). *Faith of the Fatherless*. San Francisco: Ignatius Press. P. 156. For the emotional aspects of Marx's atheism.

251 Karl Marx. Retrieved from http://www.quotationspage.com/ quotes/Karl_Marx.

252 Paul Vitz (2013). *Faith of the Fatherless*. San Francisco: Ignatius Press. P. 65-66. For the emotional aspects of Freud's atheism.

253 Sigmund Freud. Retrieved from http://www.quotationspage. com/quotes/Sigmund_Freud.

254 Eugenics movement. Retrieved from https://en.wikipedia.org/ wiki/Eugenics

255 Paul Vitz (2013). *Faith of the Fatherless*. San Francisco: Ignatius Press. P. 136-137. For the emotional aspects of Hitler's interest in atheistic philosophers.

256 Adolf Hitler. Retrieved from en.m.wikipedia.org.

257 Maximillian Kolbe. Retrieved from en.m.wikipedia.org.

258 Paul Vitz (2013). *Faith of the Fatherless*. San Francisco: Ignatius Press. P. 134-136. For the emotional aspects of Stalin's atheism.

259 Josef Stalin. Retrieved from en.m.wikipedia.org.

260 Paul Vitz (2013). *Faith of the Fatherless*. San Francisco: Ignatius Press. P.137-138. For the emotional aspects of Mao's atheism.

261 Mao Zedong. Retrieved from en.m.wikipedia.org.

262　For example, Pope Leo XIII (1878). *Quod Apostolici Muneris* (On socialism). Retrieved from http://www.ewtn.com/library/ENCYC/L13APOST.htm. The Biblical gift of prophecy is exemplified here as an ancient form of testable predictions from natural law (e.g. Deuteronomy 18:22).

Cf. Fred Hoyle (1983). *The Intelligent Universe*. London: Michael Joseph (pp.9 and 251), where he predicts self-destruction of the nihilistic culture.

263　Dostoevsky (1878). Retrieved from http://www.the-philosopy.com/god-exist-permitted-dostoevsky

264　Maximillian Kolbe. Retrieved from en.m.wikipedia.org.

265　Catherine of Siena and the Black Death. Retrieved from http://www.christianitytoday.com/history/issues/issue-30/black-death.html and Rodney Stark (1996). *The Rise of Christianity: How the Obscure, Marginal Jesus Movement Became the Dominant Religious Force in the Western World in a Few Centuries*. Princeton, NJ: Princeton University Press. Pp. 82-90. Stark studies two great plagues during the Roman Empire and documents how many Christians defied infection and death to provide nursing care to Christians and pagans… "pagan communities did not match Christian levels of benevolence during the epidemics." P. 84.

266　St. Francis kissed a leper. Retrieved from http://www.vatican.va/spirit/documents/spirit_20001103_tom-da-celano_en.html

267　Father Damian and the lepers. Retrieved from https://en.wikipedia.org/wiki/Father_Damien

268　Arthur Brooks (2006). *Who Really Cares? America's Charity Divide—Who Gives, Who Doesn't and Why It Matters*. NY: Basic Books.

269　Ibid., pp. 12-13.

270　Ibid., p. 34.

271　Koenig, Larson and McCullough (2001). *Handbook of Religion and Health*. NY: Oxford Press.

272 Anonymous (2006). *Unprotected: A Campus Psychiatrist Reveals How Political Correctness in Her Profession Endangers Every Student*. NY: Penguin Group. P. 50. (Later printings name "Anonymous"—Dr. Miriam Grossman)

273 Koenig, Larson and McCullough (2000). *Handbook of Religion and Health*. P. 325.

274 Koenig, Larson and McCullough (2000). *Handbook of Religion and Health*. P. 324.

275 Stephen Meyer (2004). "The origin of biological information and the higher taxonomic categories." *Proceedings of the Biological Society of Washington*. Volume 117 (2) (August 2004) Pp. 213-239.

276 Ben Stein (2008). *Expelled*. DVD Documentary produced by Premise Media Corporation and Vivendi Entertainment. Universal City, California.

277 Stephen Hawking (1988). *A Brief History of Time*. NY: Bantam Books. P. 149. Cf. Thaxton, Bradley and Olson (1984) *The Mystery of Life's Origin*. Dallas: Lewis and Stanley. Pp. 118 and 121. "Entropy arrow".

278 Ben Stein (2008). *Expelled*. DVD Documentary produced by Premise Media Corporation and Vivendi Entertainment. Universal City, California.

279 Francis Collins (2006). *The Language of God*. NY: Simon and Schuster. P. 91. Cf. Fred Hoyle (1983). *The Intelligent Universe*. London: Michael Joseph. (P. 160)

Notes to Chapter 7: Sister Water, Brothers Wind, Air and Fire

280 Classical Element. Retrieved from en.m.wikipedia.org

281 How long can a person survive without food? Retrieved from https:/www.scientificamerican.com

282 Atmosphere of earth. Retrieved from en.m.wikipedia.org.

283 What is the atmosphere like on other planets? Retrieved from https:/www.universetoday.com.

284 Greenhouse gas. Retrieved from en.m.wikipedia.org.

285 Photosynthesis. Retrieved from en.m.wikipedia.org.

286 Ruminants. Retrieved from en.m.wikipedia.org

287 Frances Moore Lappe' (1971/1984). *Diet for a Small Planet*. NY: Ballantine Books. P. 74-75.

288 Nitrogen fixation. Retrieved from en.m.wikipedia.org.

289 Ibid.

290 Ibid.

291 How meat and poultry fit in your healthy diet. Retrieved from https://www.mayoclinic.org/healthy-lifestyle/nutrition-and-healthy-eating/in-depth/food-and-nutrition/art-20048095

292 Koenig, Larson and McCullough (2000). *Handbook of Religion and Health*. P. 362 on longevity of Seventh Day Adventists (who are vegetarians).

293 Frances Moore Lappe (1984). *Diet for a small Planet*. Ballantine Books. Pp. 74-77.

294 Ibid.

295 Ibid., P. 69-71.

296 The Footprint of Meat. *National Geographic* (November, 2014)

297 Cattle production of methane gas. Retrieved from https://www.theguardian.com/environment/2014/jul/21/giving-up-beef-reduce-carbon-footprint-more-than-cars

298 Frances Moore Lappe (1971/1984). *Diet for a small Planet*. Ballantine Books. Pp. 78-81

299 Ibid., Pp. 78-81. Appendix D. provides tables of complementary proteins in grains and legumes.

300 Dal. Retrieved from en.m.wikipedia.org.

301 Frances Moore Lappe (1971/1984). *Diet for a small Planet*. Ballantine Books. P. 172.

302 Atmosphere of earth. Retrieved from en.m.wikipedia.org.

303 Retrieved from oceaninstitute.org

304 Body water. Retrieved from en.m.wikipedia.org.

305 Why does ice float in water? George Zaidan and Charles Morton TED-ed. www.youtube.com

306 Can humans drink Seawater? Retrieved from www.oceanservice.noaa.gov

Notes to Chapter 8: Brother Pain

307 Theodicy. Retrieved from https://en.wikipedia.org/wiki/Theodicy

308 Paul Brand and Philip Yancey (1993, 1997). *The Gift of Pain*. Grand Rapids, MI: Zondervan Press.

309 Harold Kushner (1981). *When Bad Things Happen to Good People*. NY: Random House. Pp. 70-71. Also, Tony Dungy's son had "congenital insensitivity to pain" Tony Dungy (2007). *Quiet Strength*. IL: Tynedale House Publishers. P. 181.

310 Reduced muscle mass, strength and performance in space. Retrieved from en.m.wikipedia.org.

311 Retrieved from https://www.menshealth.com/fitness/astronaut-fitness

312 How to help a butterfly out of a cocoon (by Kimberlee Leonard). Retrieved from sciencing.com.

313 Roma Downey (2018). *Box of Butterflies*. NY: Howard Books. P.46.

314 Palliative Care. Retrieved from en.m.wikipedia.org.

315 Hospice. Retrieved from en.m.wikipedia.org.

316 Victor Frankl (1946). *Man's Search for Meaning*. Cutchogue,NY: Buccaneer books.

317 Robert Cardinal Sarah (2017). *The Power of Silence*. San Francisco: Ignatius Press. P. 92. Cf. Rabbi Harold Kushner on God's suffering (1981). *When Bad Things Happen to Good People*. P. 94.

318 Lumen Gentium (para.34) in *Vatican Council II: The Conciliar and Post-Conciliar Documents*. Austin Flannery, ed. (1975) NY: Costello Publishing Company.

319 Cardinal Robert Sarah (p. 92). Cf. Rabbi Harold Kushner (p. 94)

Notes to Chapter 9: Sister Death

320 Roman Empire. Retrieved from en.m.wikipedia.org.

321 Compare "The Parable of the Twins" by "an unknown author" in Mark Link (1991). *Path Through Catholicism*. Allen, Texas: Tabor Publishing. P. 89.

322 Cambrian explosion. Retrieved from en.m.wikipedia.org.

323 Satellite delay. Retrieved from en.m.wikipedia.org.

324 www.SKYPE.com

325 www.Facetime.com

326 Teilhard de Chardin, 1955. The English Edition, *Phenomenon of Man*, was first published in 1959. NY: Harper and Row. pp. 180-181.

327 Beatific vision. Retrieved from en.m.wikipedia.org.

328 Raymond Moody (1976). *Life after Life*. Harrisburg, PA: Stackpole Books

329 Ibid., p. 92.

330 Ibid., p. 56.

331 Melvin Morse (1990). *Closer to the Light*. NY: Random House.

332 *Breakthrough* (2019). Twentieth Century Fox

333 Eben Alexander (2012). *Proof of Heaven*. NY: Simon and Schuster.

334 Some recent examples: "Teen with severe brain damage regains consciousness after parents decide to donate his organs." Retrieved from http://www.nydailynews.com/news/national/teen-regains-consciousness-parents-opt-donate-organs-article-1.3975358 . "The story behind a vegetative patient's shocking recovery." Retrieved from http://www.macleans.ca/society/health/

the-story-behind-a-vegetative-patients-shocking-re-covery/ . "Trapped in his body for 12 years, a man breaks free." Retrieved from http://www.npr.org/sections/health-shots/2015/01/09/376084137/trapped-in-his-body-for-12-years-a-man-breaks-free . Fred Hoyle (1983). *The Intelligent Universe*. London: Michael Joseph. "...many of us have the instinctive feeling that the software—ourselves—might have an existence independent of the hardware—our bodies." (p. 225)

335 Dying declaration. Retrieved from en.m.wikipedia.org.

336 Bartholomew the Apostle. Tradition Retrieved from en.m.wiki-pedia.org.

337 Rodney Stark (1996/1997). *The Rise of Christianity*. San Francisco: HarperCollins. Pp. 187-188.

338 Lee Strobel (2008). *The Case for Christ: A Journalist's Personal Investigation of the Evidence for Jesus*. Grand Rapids, MI: Zondervan

339 *Josephus: Complete Works* (1960/1981). *Antiquities of the Jews*. Book 18, Chapter 3, para. 3. William Whiston, trans. Grand Rapids, MI: Kregel Publications.

Notes to Chapter 10: Mortal Sin and the Second Death

340 Hedonism is the name of an ancient philosophy grounded in the selfish pursuit of maximum pleasure.

341 Objectivism. Retrieved from en.m.wikipedia.org.

342 Ayn Rand. Philosophy. Retrieved from en.m.wikipedia.org.

343 Hedonism. Retrieved from en.m.wikipedia.org.

344 Eugenics. History. Retrieved from en.m.wikipedia.org.

345 Margaret Sanger. Views. Eugenics. Retrieved from en.m.wiki-pedia.org.

346 Retrieved from: http://www.uscatholic.org/articles/201501/what-preferential-option-poor-29649

347 Karl Menninger (1973). *Whatever Became of Sin?* NY: Hawthorn Books.

348 For a good summary of the Teilhard controversy and references by recent Popes Paul VI, John Paul II, Benedict XVI and Francis, see H. Reed Armstrong (Nov. 27, 2017). Teilhard de Chardin: The Vatican II Architect you need to know. Retrieved from https://onepeterfive.com/teilhard-chardin-vii-architect/.

349 Richard Dawkins (1976/2006). *The Selfish Gene.* NY: Oxford University Press.

350 *Catechism of the Catholic Church* (CCC). Part 1, section 2, chapter 2, article 5, number 631ff. retrieved from www.vatican.va.

351 Rodney Stark (1996). *The Rise of Christianity: How the obscure, marginal Jesus Movement became the dominant force in the western world in a few centuries.* NJ: Princeton University Press.

352 List of religious populations. Retrieved from en.m.wikipedia.org.

353 Francis Collins (2006). *The Language of God.* NY: Simon and Schuster. P. 90.

354 Ibid., p. 93.

355 Ibid., pp. 28-29. Cf. Fred Hoyle (1983). *The Intelligent Universe.* London: Michael Joseph. Fred is impressed with a similar theory attributed to Alfred Russell Wallace: "The utilitarian hypothesis, which is the theory of natural selection applied to mind", he wrote, "seems inadequate to account for the development of the moral sense…how can we believe that considerations of utility could ever invest [the moral sense] with the mysterious sanctity of the highest virtue—could ever induce men to value truth for its own sake, and practice it regardless of consequences?" (p. 233).

356 Francis Collins (2006). *The Language of God.* NY: Simon and Schuster. P. 27

357 Ibid., p. 23.

358 The Declaration of Independence. Retrieved from ushis-tory.org.

359 List of religious populations. Retrieved from en.m.wiki-pedia.org.

360 Christianity in the United States. Retrieved from en.m.wiki-pedia.org.

361 Code of Hammurabi. Retrieved from en.m.wikipedia.org.

362 Ibid.

363 613 commandments. Retrieved from en.m.wikipedia.org

364 Code of Hammurabi. Retrieved from en.m.wikipedia.org

365 Kuhn, Thomas (1996) *The Structure of Scientific Revolutions*. University of Chicago Press.

366 Pope John Paul II coined the phrase "culture of death" in his encyclical Evangelium vitae (April 1995). Retrieved from "Culture of Life" en.m.wikipedia.org.

367 Rodney Stark (1996/1997). *The Rise of Christianity*. San Francisco: HarperCollins. P.117. p.121.

368 Europe needs many more babies to avert a population disaster. Retrieved from https://www.theguardian.com/world/2015/aug/23/baby-crisis-europe-brink-depopulation-disaster?CMP=share_btn_link

369 *Humani Vitae*: On the regulation of human births. Pope Paul VI (1968). Retrieved from www.papalencyclicals.net. The Biblical gift of prophecy is exemplified here as an ancient form of test-able predictions from natural law (e.g. Deuteronomy 18:22).

370 Barash and Lipton (2009). *How women got their curves*. NY: Columbia University Press. p. 158.

371 Ibid., p. 147.

372 Ibid., p. 148.

373 Ibid., p. 118.

374 John Paul II (Cardinal Karol Wojtyla) (1981/1993). *Love and Responsibility*. San Francisco: Ignatius Press. P.272. See

also John Paul II (1997). Theology of the Body. Boston: Pauline Books. Eg. Pp.378ff.

375 Inbreeding. Retrieved from en.m.wikipedia.org.

376 J.M. Cohen, ed. (1969). *Christopher Columbus*. NY: Penguin Books. P. 18.

377 Miriam Grossman (2006/2007). *Unprotected*. NY: Penguin Group (USA) Inc. p.23.

378 W.H.O. Says 40 Million Will Be Infected With AIDS Virus by 2000. Retrieved from https://partners.nytimes.com/library/national/science/aids/061891sci-aids.html Actual numbers retrieved from: https://www.wolframalpha.com/input/?i=AIDs+deaths+worldwide

379 Is Casual Sex Fulfilling? Not so much, According to this Millennial. Retrieved from http://dailysignal.com/2017/09/21/casual-sex-fulfilling-not-much-according-millennial/

380 Miriam Grossman (2006/2007). *Unprotected*. NY: Penguin Group (USA) Inc. p.22.

381 Magna Carta. Retrieved from en.m.wikipedia.org.

382 Universal Declaration of Human Rights. United Nations (1948). Retrieved from http://www.unhchr.ch/udhr/lang/eng_print.htm

383 Universal Declaration of Human Rights. Retrieved from https://en.wikipedia.org/wiki/Universal_Declaration_of_Human_Rights

384 Robert Spitzer (2010). *New Proofs for the Existence of God*. Pp. 48. Cf. Fred Hoyle (1983). *The Intelligent Universe*. London: Michael Joseph (p. 168) "the most incomprehensible thing about the Universe is that it is comprehensible at all." (quoting Einstein)

385 Pope Leo XIII (see note 262). Cf. Fred Hoyle (1983). *The Intelligent Universe*. London: Michael Joseph (pp.9 and 251) where he predicts the self-destruction of nihilistic cultures.

386 Koenig, Larson and McCullough (2001). *Handbook of Religion and Health*. NY: Oxford Press.

Notes to Epilogue: God Speaks

387 Robert Spitzer (2010). *New Proofs for the Existence of God*. Grand Rapids, MI: William B. Eerdmans. Pp. 59-60.

388 Ibid., p. 60.

389 Ibid., p. 59.

390 Ibid., p. 63.

391 Ibid., p. 64.

392 Ibid., p.64.

393 Stephen Meyer (2009). *Signature in the Cell: DNA and the Evidence for Intelligent Design.* NY: Harper Collins. p.11-12

394 Francis Collins (2006). *The Language of God*. NY: Simon and Schuster.

395 Ibid., pp.122-123.

396 John of the Cross (2003). *Dark Night of the Soul*. Westminster, Maryland: The Newman Press.

397. Pascal's Wager. Retrieved from en.m.wikipedia.org

Letters to God from Teens with Jobe Syndrome

Dear God,

I've messed up this year. I've been through a lot of stuff and I was wondering why did you let me go through all those problems? I mean, you want me to believe in you, but you haven't made me happy. You took my grandmother away from me, my mother is gone, my dad is gone. How could I believe in you when you let all this stuff happen to me? God, I'm kinda mixed up right now because I don't know who to believe in. So, whoever you are, would you come and save me from my problems? Please help me and my family.

Dear God,
I'm not in the mood to talk. That's why I am not going to write anything. Get back with you later.

Dear God,
I'm writing you this letter to say can you show me some ways that I can do because you say ask and it shall be given unto you, seek and you shall find, knock and the door will be open

unto you. I have knocked and I don't think the door was opened. I have seek and I did not find and I have asked and I don't think it was heard. So could you do something about it because I do think you said I didn't send My Son to condemn the world, but to save the world.

Dear God,
I don't believe you because every time I ask you to do something it don't never happen. And another thing, if you was so real you wouldn't have let that happen to my mother and plus I be asking you to show me something that you know that my mother is doing all right. It don't never happen.

Dear God,
I don't believe. I've lived for 16 years and haven't seen any proof. I really can't say that everything always goes bad, but the things that I usually like are wrong and I get locked up for it. I can't trust anyone that I know, so how can I trust you? Sometimes I feel like giving up and dying cause this life ain't nothing. I can't see myself making nothing out of myself. I look at my life and I wish I had better. But then I still kind of like what I do or did. I guess I'm used to it. I've did a lot to people and I just want it to be over. I know my time will come. I just don't want to fool myself by trying to make it and then jump back into the old ways and fail.

Dear Allah,
I don't like you anymore. The reason why is because you took my parents away from me. I really don't want to have anything to do with you. I feel that you are a demon god, and you only wish bad things to happen to me and to others who worship

you. I really don't have much to say, I really don't know what to believe, but I guess I brought it on myself.

Dear Lord Jesus Christ,
I've been having a lot of problems and I need your help. I'm asking you to forgive me for my sins. I want to accept you in my heart as my Lord and savior, but there are a lot of things that I do that are against your rules. I really want your help, but not at this moment. I'm having a lot of difficulties at this time, and I need your help, but I don't want it right now because of some of the things that I want to do. But believe me, at this rate I'm going to need it sooner than I want to.

Dear Big Fella,
I don't really understand stuff. Why didn't you let me die? Why? Because if you would have, the people at Boysville wouldn't have never knew me and I wouldn't hurt my family and friends. I just don't understand why would you let me put people through more pain. Why don't you just stop me from living? It will stop me from hurting people and people won't start caring, and when I do stuff I'll hurt people. Like 2 of my staff members said, I have a good heart but don't know how to show them. But I ask you this, what is my purpose on earth? I haven't found out.

P.S. You don't mind if I call you Big Fella?

Dear God or Jesus,
I want you to forgive me for all the stuff I did. I should have asked you to forgive me then, but I never thought about it. I wanted it and probably did want to give up on you because I

used to think that if you wanted to have a perfect world, then why do you let all this stuff happen to us and everybody else?

Dear Big Fella,
What's up? How are you? Me, I'm having problems in my life. Having dreams. Not saying how I really feel. I don't really know how to say stuff. I believe there's something. Why did you let my mother treat me like that? Why did you let me go off like that and hurt people? I really don't understand why all this stuff happens to me. What are more things I can do to become a better person? Why do I always hate myself? Why don't I act like regular people? If you can help, let's talk. Every time I try to stop writing, I can't, because ore things come up in my head. I don't know how to say stuff because I'm a 17 year old man. I'm still a big kid inside, and I don't know how to show things. I don't know how to show people that I care about them. Teach me ___why. Help me become a better person. I love you but I don't know how to show my love for others, not even you. How do I cry? I do. I say stuff. I need help and the people I care about. I want you to tell C,F,L,J,N,J,O, Mr. C, Mr. M, Ms. J, Ms. L keep trying.

Dear God,
Forgive me for all my sins I committed today. Thank you Lord, for letting me have a good day and keeping me out of trouble. Let a thousand angels protect over me and my family and all my friends and their families. Let me have a good day tomorrow and guide me the right way and not the wrong. In Jesus name I pray. Amen. And let me give my mama a chance.

Jobe Syndrome Protocol

Problem: Anger at God / disappointment with God / alienation from God

Goal: Youth (or parent or family member) will reconcile conflicted relationship with God

Objectives	Interventions
1. The client will admit to the Chaplain his/her anger/ disappointment with God	1.1 Chaplain will explore youth's disappointment/anger at God.
	1.2 Chaplain will affirm / give permission for client to express anger at God
2. The client will identify his / her "spiritual pain".	2.1 Chaplain will explore "spiritual pain" behind anger.
3. The client will identify Biblical support for his/her anger/disappointment with God	3.1 Chaplain will discuss Job's anger at God and affirmation from God
4. The client will pray the "anger" psalms.	4.1 Chaplain will pray the lament/despair/anger Psalms with youth (or family member) (Ps. 3, 10, 13, 22, 38, 42, 44, 51, 69, 74, 88, 102, 109, 142)

5: The client will write his/ her own psalm.	5.1 Chaplain will assist the youth /family member to compose a psalm of lament and pray it with them.
6: The client will identify biblical support for a new image of God	6.1 Chaplain will provide a survey of scripture verses on God's love.
7. The client will identify God's pain and sadness/ suffering and weeping over evil	7.1 Chaplain will discuss stories of God's suffering over the client's suffering.
8. The client will identify the voice of conscience as the voice of God, trying to stop abusive behavior.	8.1 Chaplain will discuss God's use of conscience as a deterrent from evil.

Spiritual Pathway 3 (cont.)

Objectives	Interventions
9. The client will identify situations where peoples' evil decisions are the cause of pain and suffering	9.1 Chaplain will teach the concept of God having given up control over people's decisions
10. The client will identify at least three different answers to prayer (yes, no, and not yet)	10.1 Chaplain will discuss why God doesn't always say "yes" to our prayers.
	10.2 Chaplain will discuss how God answered "no" to Jesus' prayer in Gethsemane.
	10.3 Chaplain will discuss Jesus' prayer (Psalm 22) on the cross
11. The client will identify situations where good people experience pain and suffering	11.1 Chaplain will witness to his/ her own pain and suffering
	11.2 Chaplain will teach the concept of the mystery of evil/suffering as unknowable.

	11.3 Chaplain will offer readings on the topic. (*For example: When bad things happen to good people* (Kushner)*; Disappointment with God* (Yancey).)
	11.4 Chaplain will teach the concept of Redemptive Suffering as meaningful.
12. Client will express reconciliation with God.	12.1 Chaplain prays with client for reconciliation with God.

The Logic of the Arguments

1. Eternal universe vs the Big Bang theories
   - If the universe (and life) were eternal, it would now be at maximum entropy
   - But the entropy value of the universe (and living things) is very low
   - Then the universe (and life) must not be eternal (it had a beginning)

2. Eternal universe vs the Big Bang theories
   - The universe is either eternal without a first cause, or it had a beginning with a first cause
   - The universe exploded from the Big Bang about 14 billion years ago
   - The universe had a beginning and a first cause

3. Entropy and evolution
   - Entropy is a measure of chaos, disorder and simplicity
   - The 2nd law of thermodynamics states that all natural processes inevitably proceed from order and complexity to disorder and simplicity (entropy naturally increases)

- Evolution theory claims that, by means of mutation and natural selection, the random, chaotic simplicity of inanimate chemicals evolved into a multitude of animals, plants and humans—highly complex and ordered and living things.
- Evolution theory contradicts the 2nd law of thermodynamics

4. Entropy and Intelligent Design
   - Only highly intelligent beings can design complex machines from chemicals
   - Evolution naturally selects simple chemicals to produce complex machines
   - Evolution must be designed by an intelligent being

5. Machines and Intelligent Design
   - The existence of complex machines is evidence of Intelligent Design
   - Living cells, human brains, computers and watches are complex machines
   - Cells, human brains, computers, and watches are evidence of Intelligent Design

6. DNA and Intelligent Design (Stephen Meyer, pp 378-379)
   - Despite a thorough search, no material causes have been discovered that demonstrate the power to produce large amounts of specified information
   - Intelligent causes have demonstrated the power to produce large amounts of specified information
   - Intelligent design constitutes the best, most causally adequate, explanation for the information in the cell

7. DNA and Intelligent Design
    - Language and messages are evidence for Intelligent Design
    - DNA is a language and messages
    - DNA is evidence for Intelligent Design

8. DNA and Supreme Intelligence
    - The complexity of a message is a measure of intelligence
    - DNA encodes extremely complex messages (3 billion words in human DNA)
    - DNA is evidence for a Supreme Intelligence

9. Anthropy and probability
    - A universe that has 20 physical constant numbers that happen to be precisely valued to produce living cells and intelligent humans is extremely improbable
    - Our universe has produced living cells and intelligent humans
    - Our universe is extremely improbable.

10. Anthropy and Intelligent Design
    - All of the physical constants in the universe are finely-tuned to produce and support life on Mother Earth.
    - Fine-tuning is evidence for the existence of a Fine-Tuner/ Intelligent Designer
    - The universe was created by a Supreme Intelligence

11. Altruism vs. Selfishness
    - Evolution theory includes natural selection of the fittest forms of life and is an intrinsically selfish process denying the existence of altruism/ selflessness/agape

- Saints are honored for their altruism/unselfishness/agape love
- Evolution cannot explain the existence of altruism/selflessness/agape love

12. Original Sin and Selfishness
   - Theologians have called selfish actions "sin"
   - Evolution theory includes natural selection of the fittest forms of life and is an intrinsically selfish process (The Selfish Gene)
   - The first humans' actions were selfish
   - The first humans committed the "Original Sin"

13. Moral order and physical order
   - If there is a moral order in the universe, then intelligent humans should have discovered it, just like they have discovered physical laws
   - Most human cultures have laws against murder, adultery, theft and perjury
   - There must be a moral order in the universe

14. Moral order and the Existence of God
   - There is either a Supreme Being sanctioning the moral order or I am alone among my peers with moral chaos and the "survival of the fittest" person, gang or state
   - I can hear the voice of the Supreme Being in my mind/conscience
   - There is a Supreme Being sanctioning the moral order

15. Moral order and the Existence of God
    - Either God exists and sanctions a moral order of justice or God does not exist and natural selection—survival of the fittest—is the only moral order among humans
    - God exists
    - Survival of the fittest violates the moral order of justice among humans

16. Moral order and Existence of God
    - "If God does not exist, anything is permissible" (Dostoevsky)
    - Joseph Stalin and Mao Zedong believed God does not exist
    - Stalin and Mao Zedong believed execution of 20+ million civilians was permissible

17. The Supreme Being and life expectancy
    - If there is a moral order and a Benevolent Supreme Being, then religious people should be healthier than non-religious people
    - The relative hazard of dying was reduced by 46% for frequent Churchgoers in one study
    - Then there must be a moral order and a Benevolent Supreme Being

18. The Supreme Being and Charity
    - If there is a moral order and a Benevolent Supreme Being, then religious people should be more generous in giving to charity than non-religious people.
    - Religious people gave 3.5 times more money to charity than non-religious people in one study (they also volunteered more than twice as often)

- Then there must be a moral order and Supreme Being

19. Bio- field/soul and life
    - All objects on earth are either collections of inanimate atoms and molecules or they are collections of animated cells
    - If they are animated cells, then they possess something that the inanimate collections do not possess
    - Let's call that something, the cell-field, the bio-field or the soul

20. Bio-field /soul and the Primordial Soup
    - If there is a perfect blend of atoms and molecules present in two separate suspensions, one in a primordial soup and the other in a living cell, one is inanimate and the other animate
    - There is no known biochemical difference in the two sets of atoms and molecules
    - Science cannot explain the origin of life

21. Biofield/soul: the Fifth force field
    - "All forces are transmitted by fields" (Hawking, 2010, p. 89)
    - The living cell is animated by a field not among the four known fields
    - There must be a fifth, a bio-field or a soul, animating the living cell

22. Relativism vs Objective truth
    - Relativists claim that no one can be certain that their claims are true for everyone
    - Relativists claim that their claim is true for everyone

- Relativists cannot be certain that their claim is true for everyone, and
- Objectivists claims could be true

23. Relativism vs Objectivism
    - Relativists claim that there is no objective order in the universe
    - But science has discovered an abundance of order in the universe
    - Relativists are wrong

24. The Problem of Pain
    - If there is a meaning and purpose for pain, then the Intelligent Designer is also Benevolent
    - Pain protects organs from serious injuries
    - The Intelligent Designer is also Benevolent

25. The Problem of Death
    - If Death is the end of life, then death is evil.
    - But death is not the end of life; it is a birth into paradise
    - Death is not evil.

Index

CPSIA information can be obtained
at www.ICGtesting.com
Printed in the USA
FSHW021403210421
80653FS